You can contribute to support the pro␣ ␣␣␣␣␣ ␣ about in this book.

Please visit:

www.yourpal-steve.org

And

www.solutionbeaconfoundation.org

for more information.

All profits from the sale and distribution of this publication are used to support the Peifers' programs and mission.

-- *The Solution Beacon Foundation*
December 2005

Compiled and edited by Alicia Hoekstra

Your Pal, Steve

Steve Peifer

Solution Beacon Foundation
P.O, Box 386
Wray, CO 80758 USA

Send feedback, inquiries, or special requests to:
SBFoundation@solutionbeacon.net

Your Pal Steve
ISBN 1-4196-2439-3
Pub Date: Dec-30-2005

To order additional copies, please contact:

BookSurge, LLC
www.booksurge.com
1-800-308-6235
Orders@booksurge.com

Table of Contents

Your Pal, Steve

In memory of

Stephen Wrigley Peifer
March 1998

Though his days on this earth were few,
his brief life still touches many

Your Pal, Steve

Don't be Afraid of the Storms

On May 1st, 2001, the world as I knew it ended. I lost my mother long before her time. All that was good and right with the world went with her. It was the darkest time of my life. No hope, no joy, no happiness, only an unbearable pain that seemed to never end.

She was my best friend.

She was the foundation for all my successes throughout my life.

She was the rock and my safe haven when I failed.

She never judged and was always there for me.

On September 11, 2001, I finally understood why she had left me so early. But it did not make it any easier to keep going.

Along with her constant smile and unqualified love, the one thing I remember most is she used to sing me to sleep with the song "You'll Never Walk Alone" and my favorite line from the song was "Hold your head up high and don't be afraid of the storms."

When she went to sleep with the angels and the storms seemed to be overwhelming me, Steve's letters kept me going even when it did not seem possible. He shared his family, his hope, his faith, his joy and amazements, his accomplishments and defeats without complaint or regrets even though he himself was dealing with the unbearable loss of his son. And, in addition to the letters, he did something for me that I'll never be able to repay.

He built the first ever solar-powered computer center in the middle of Kenya and named it after my mom. Her good acts towards everyone during her life will live on long after we are all gone.

He saved my life.

I'm not afraid of the storms anymore. My pal Steve gave me hope and light again through his faith in God and humanity.

You'll never be afraid or walk alone again. Now, he's your pal as well.

John Stouffer
Dallas, Texas
December 2005

Letters from 2000

Africa Never Lets You Forget

What is the vilest insult a ten-year-old boy can hurl at another ten-year-old boy? If you say `Hey, you stink' there is usually agreement and the opportunity to talk about the favorite subject, which is gas. Recently, one of our guys had a birthday. In our house on birthdays, we like to go around and state what we like about that person. One guy said `I like that he is handsome to girls.' With great fury, the accused said `I am not. You are.' He replied `Only to my mother, and she's not a real girl.' Then a theological discussion ensued regarding whether mothers are girls or exactly what they are. The debate ended, somehow like all of them do, discussing the most exciting thing to hit campus so far this year.

The Pinewood Derby has begun. It is really really big here. You get a block of wood about the size of your hand, and you begin to mold a car from it. I have guys in the dorm that can never get out of bed in the morning, but are up before I call them sanding and thinking about great designs that will gain them speed. Little boys, power tools and cars: can life get any better?

Some old friends have reminded me of the award I won in college when I went to an African American bar and won the `Whitest boy on the planet' for my dancing. Somehow the fact that I have ended up in Africa pales in comparison to the fact that I am one of the helpers in the Pinewood Derby. Wood and I don't get along; it is ugly to me so I try to hurt it. I once built a birdhouse and the left side came out; I hammered it and the right side came out. So I did the logical thing and hit both sides: the top flew off and I am convinced I got a B in shop class because of the joy I gave to the instructor. The good news is that I have a son JT who is gifted in such things, and my design will include writing on the body that says things like `Thank God Almighty for the wonderful judges.'

Africa never lets you forget you are in Africa. Nan got a call to come down to the hospital to give blood for a baby. As she went to give it, the Kenyan nurse remarked to Nan that most Africans couldn't give blood; it isn't rich enough because of their diets.

We had another reminder this week. In the states, we would have a garden because it was fun and because we wanted real tomatoes. In Africa, if your garden doesn't come in, it is that much less food you eat. So many people here are hungry, because their gardens haven't come in due to the drought.

It puts such tremendous pressure on folks. There is no free education for children in Africa; if you can't pay; your children are pulled out of school until you can pay. Do you spend the money on food or education? What a horrible, grievous choice, and the reality for so many people here.

In the church service today, a pastor brought up 5 street boys; ages 8-12. They were abandoned or their parents died of Aids. So they are left to the streets; there is no government agency to take care of them, and so many of them end on the streets and start sniffing glue to forget their misery. One was the same age as Matthew, who was in my lap, and I couldn't take my eyes off of him. You can never get away from the tremendous need in Africa: Africa never lets you forget.

Your old pal,

Steve

And Then There Were Ten... Wait – Make That Nine

We are dorm parents, and we had our ten 10 year old boys come this week. There are four Koreans, one Indian, one national, and three Americans, although two of the Americans have spent more time in Africa than America. The first night was rather traumatic; lots of tears and lots of trying not to have tears, because ten-year-old boys don't cry no matter what nationality they are.

The differences between nationality in ten year old boys are this: they all list pizza as their favorite food, but the Koreans like pizza and noodles. Otherwise, there seems to be universality to 10 year olds. Much of it centers on gas. Ten-year-old boys, when they are in a group, talk about gas in a way that no other age group does. They take gas seriously: a discussion on Thursday involved whether if they hooked tubes to their bottoms and connected it to the stove, could you cook with it? This was not a discussion to provoke mirth; it was serious. A passing discussion later asked the question: `Is it true that the first time you kiss a girl you go home and throw up?' One response that I heard was `I don't know if you have to, but I know that I'm gonna'. Again, this was not said to be funny.

This school is boy heaven; they live across the street from the school, a huge playground and the soccer field. There are lots of trees to climb, and all your pals live within five minutes. But it means being separated from your parents, and that is tough. One guy cried in our bedroom for two hours, and most of it was because he felt like this was not a way for a big guy to act. We are constantly telling them it's OK to be sad, but how many ways can you prove you are tough when you are ten than by not crying? They all seem to being doing better, except for:

Our tenth guy, Andrew, came to school on Monday. He was not feeling good, so he was taken to the doctor. After five minutes, the doctor said `we are going to remove the appendix today.' Whenever you feel like you've been given a tough break, think about this 10 year old from North Carolina who is going to be away from his folks for the first time, which is tough enough, but to have your appendix removed in an African hospital. He was brave, and he is doing fine, but visiting him at the hospital was sobering.

The doctor was great; he is a professor at Stanford and a world-renowned surgeon. But the hospital is shocking to a westerner. The floors were filthy, and the smell horrible. While I was visiting him, he was given water in a glass that had pink medicine on its outside. I don't understand why it is like this, but I am assured by many that this is one of the finest hospitals in Africa.

Andrew has tested out of fifth grade, so he has moved to the sixth grade dorm. That leaves us nine, but we have not experienced a drop off in noise at this point. On Saturday, we had a baboon walk across our front porch and look in our garbage can. I'm not sure this was as alarming as hosting an ice cream party for all the fifth grade boys later that night and having the power go off. Power outages are a fact of life here, but it is a different thing to have power off with that many 10 year olds. We survived, but I'll take my chances with the baboon next time.

Happy Labor Day!

Your old pal,

Steve

Attack of the Hungry Baboons!

I had a defining moment this week.

But before I get to that, there were other things of note:

1. We went to the dukas to eat. Dukas are restaurants within walking distance. Their walls are made of tin, and the one we ate at was deluxe; it had a cement floor rather than a dirt one. There was a large menu on the wall. It was primarily for decoration, for you soon learn it is better to ask `What do you have?' than request different items that they don't have. Chickens regularly walked in and out of the restaurant. Coke, which is ubiquitous in Africa, is served from the bottle and is warm. A friend from here swears that he was in a duka and ordered chicken, and the cook grabbed a chicken that walked in the door and prepared it as they watched. The food was good, but we didn't order chicken,

2. A group of us went to Nakuru National Park. It is a large park, almost 40 miles in total size. You can drive around on its unpaved roads and see rhino's, flamingos, warthogs, lions, monkeys and baboons. After going through for several hours, we stopped to eat lunch. We were sitting in a circle when a baboon leaped in and grabbed a sandwich. Unlike many thieves, he just sat and ate it. There are several things I didn't know about baboons before I arrived in Africa; to be honest, I don't ever recall having a thought about one before I came here. But they have two-inch molars, and four of them can take on a lion, so you don't mess with them. What a common defense is is to throw stones near them; you don't want to throw at them, because that can make them mad and they will charge. They will sometimes pick up stones and throw back! So, with a stern warning to not show our teeth because that is a sign of aggression, we drove them off with stones and moved our picnic. Five minutes later, they attacked again, and grabbed potato chips, and calmly ate them while we got more stones, and drove them off. We had to stand guard so they wouldn't swipe our food for the rest of the picnic.

3. The newspaper here is called `The Nation.' There is a census going on now, and a headline will read `This census the best ever.' In the third paragraph, they will mention that 106 census takers have threatened to destroy the documents if they are not paid in full. (Incidentally, one of the questions is `How many wives do you have?') We don't have Internet access in this part of Kenya because the phone lines are so bad, but it is on line and line for line it's the most unusual read you'll have today. How many census takers in the US are injured by hippos in the line of duty? http://www.nation.co.ke

4. We went to church today down in the valley at a Masai church. It has a tin roof, dirt floors and wooden benches with no back. It was in Swahili, so much of it flew by me. But the worship was joyous, and the singing was beautiful. When they took the offering, I saw people with nothing give their tithes, and at the end of the service, our whole family was given wristbands and necklaces.

I don't know how to articulate this, but when I saw these people, most of them barefoot or in shoes that had huge holes in them giving their tithes, I felt like my whole life passed before my eyes, and I saw myself for the first time. And I didn't feel worthy to be in that place. And the truth is, I'm not worthy.

I always said I wanted to come to Africa to learn, not to teach. The kids are arriving tomorrow, and I will be teaching, but I'm learning more than I could ever teach.

Your old pal,

Steve

Untitled

August is the coldest month in the Rift Valley, so it tends to lend itself to big fires and musing on the computer. There are so many things we have seen and experienced recently, but five jump out:

1. We hired a national to help us with our firewood. His name is Fred and he is a wonderful young man, with a real heart for kids. I asked him to teach the boys to cut firewood with him. You should see our seven year old Matthew operate a panga (a large machete) or our ten year old JT swing an ax. You don't get to or need to do much of that in Texas. Fred and JT built an enclosure for:

2. Our newest pet, a three-horned chameleon that the boys have named Stevie and somehow has wormed his way into the adults' hearts. Much of the day seems to consist of rushing Stevie to one of us to note his interesting new color.

3. We asked Fred to come for dinner. In the middle of dinner, I am astonished to discover that all the usual things I like to ask someone I'm just getting to know don't work: `What is your favorite restaurant?' to someone who has eaten at a restaurant 3 times in his life; `What is your favorite movie ' to someone who doesn't have electricity, and `What are you currently reading' to someone who views books as life's sweetest luxury... I need to relearn how to make a friend.

4. On Saturday, I went with another guy down to the Valley to visit a family from the Masai tribe. It took two hours, one hour on unpaved roads. When we got there, there were three huts surrounded by thorn bushes. Simon greeted us and removed some of the bushes so we could enter.

5. The adults all shook hands; Simon lives with his wife and four children and his two brothers and their families. After the adults shook hands, the children all came and slightly bowed; I was to pat their heads. The children started rubbing my hands; Simon said that some of them had never seen a white man before. I started making funny faces, and they all giggled – kids are kids.

But I've never seen dirtier children, and children in such ragged clothing. At one point, the baby was drinking milk, and there were over thirty flies on her face. It is a sight I will never forget.

And then I was asked if I wanted to go inside the hut. It was about 5.5 tall and oval. It is made of mud and cow dung. As I stooped to enter and blinked my eyes to see, Simon motioned to the left: `That is where the calves stay at night.' Five feet to the right was where Simon and his boys slept; his wife and two daughters slept two feet away.

We brought some corn and beans, because the drought has caused some real hunger there. The problem is: how do you help people without crushing their spirits? There is a real beggar mentality in Nairobi; part of it is understandable, but part of it is how people have been helped. Remember `We are the World?' What wasn't reported was that most of the farmers lost their farms after all the food was poured into that country; nobody wanted to buy food anymore. How do you help without hurting?

Before we left for training, Nancy couldn't hold a baby without crying. In New York, she was able to start holding babies again. The healing is continuing, and we are so grateful.

We really appreciate all the email we have received; it is a real encouragement. Matthew's birthday is the 6th of September. If you have a chance, he would appreciate real mail on his birthday.

Your pal,

Steve

Beauty and the Beast

Most men that are married believe, at least deep down, that their wives are better people than they are. Guys like to scratch and spit; woman tend to be deeper and more refined. Anyway, I have always known that with my bride: she is smart, kind, and beautiful and the list can go on forever. And I am grateful for it.

But there are those rare occasions where the differences shout, and this week was one of them. We had our first week of language classes. Nan graduated with a degree in linguistics in three years. I struggle with my mother tongue. The class began, and it was obvious how gifted she was, and how amazingly unproficient I was. Our professor, Richard, is a tremendous teacher, and I am enjoying the class, but I realized that one hour into the class I began remembering an old chant from seventh grade math `Go time go. Go time go. Go go go go. Go time go.' But just like in seventh grade, it didn't help.

One day we had an assignment; go out and introduce yourself to someone, ask where he/she is from, what he or she does, and how their day has been. I, being the wise person I am, said `Can I do it in English?' After I was rebuked, I went outside and met a man named Peter. I am sure that was his name because it was on his badge. After that point, the details get fuzzy. He might work in the fields, or he might have an open sore. After I introduced myself to him, he asked me to say what I said to the two other workers, who broke out in gales of laughter. After much more interesting conversation, he put his hand on my shoulder and said `I will pray much for your Swahili teacher.'

We go to the market on Tuesday to bargain. If you discover that we have sold our house in Texas, this may be a possible explanation. Nan, on the other hand, is beginning to have real conversations with folks. Beauty and the Beast indeed...

But we saw a different side of Beauty and the Beast on Thursday. We all went to deliver maize in the valley for the famine relief effort. We had a large flatbed truck, and we delivered food to seven different churches. While we were driving across terrible roads or no roads, we saw zebras, gazelles, and other kinds of magnificent wildlife.

That is one part of Africa, but there is the Beast also. It is called the drought. We went to an orphanage, where kids are not always eating enough, and to churches where the floor is dirt and the walls don't reach the ceiling. Nan and I worked feeding the homeless in Dallas, but this is like no poverty you've seen before.

A month ago, I would look at rain and think `Now I won't get to see the game.' In three weeks, it has become `If it doesn't rain soon, lots of people are going to die.'

But what must it be like to look up at the sky and think `If it doesn't rain, I'm going to die'?

Or worse: ` If it doesn't rain, my children are going to die.'

I can't imagine. I can't even get my mind around a question like that.

I don't want to end on a down note, but I need to be honest. I wish I had answers. I just have questions.

Your old pal,

Steve

An African Thanksgiving

I've always enjoyed Thanksgiving, but its purpose for me was twofold:

- Eat until it hurts
- Eat more

We decided to invite all the singles over for the big meal. I got to come to Africa with my bride and my kids, so if I never made a friend, I would always have a good time. But I find myself marveling at people who would come all the way to Africa without any family, and have no one to come home to. They work so hard, and they give and give and give. So we didn't want any to be forgotten on this special day. And we expected a few to show up. But sometimes things take on a life of their own, and by the time it was all over, we had 27 guests. Nan made a turkey, and everyone brought something.

We had Africans, Americans, Canadians, and English folks. I tried out my newly acquired multi-cultural skills when Fred asked me what Americans were most thankful for. I told him that we were most grateful for two things:

1. We were thankful to not be in England anymore.
2. We were thankful that we didn't end up in Canada.

Nan and I have had a tradition since we were married of going around the table and telling folks why we were thankful for them. It was a wonderful time, and we are glad that this tradition transferred easily to Africa. At the end of the feast, Fred remarked that he felt like he had been to America for the first time.

`Not yet' I responded. This was the first Thanksgiving I've been away from America, and for the first time since I've been away, I found myself missing things. I've always missed family and friends and church, but Thanksgiving evoked things that surprised me; being able to just call people on the phone, the luxury of friends and family close by, newspaper ads of cool toys that I wanted for me but could give to the kids, and football. `You need to watch a football game to truly experience an American Thanksgiving' I told Fred.

I really really really wanted to watch a football game on Thanksgiving. And a dear friend offered his tapes of the Buffalo Bills to watch. But as a true Cowboys fans, the idea of watching the Bills on Thanksgiving was as enticing as kissing my sister, will all due respect to my lovely sisters. A Cowboys fan watching the Bills on Thanksgiving would feel like a commie.

And then an even dearer friend pulled out a Dallas Cowboy tape that her even dearer brother in law had sent her. And so, dreams do come true; we watched a Cowboys game during Thanksgiving. And I was amazed how much I got into the game, knowing the outcome from the beginning; I yelled with a ferocity that alarmed Grace, amused Fred, and had all the Canadians and English folks grateful that my people had made their way to America.

I have never been a particularly grateful man, but Africa has made me realize, in a new way, how much I have been given and how much I have taken for granted. I waited for 20 minutes the last time I tried to get a dial tone here; next Thanksgiving I will burn up the phone lines calling my family and friends, thanking them and apologizing for how I've taken them for granted.

Africa has helped me become grateful.

Your old pal,

Steve

Don't Get Greedy With Bunny Hops

How do you motivate young children to learn computer? A real teacher could tell you, but I'm not a real teacher, so I have had to figure it out on my own. There are three principles that have worked for me:

1. Empathy. One of the cutest first grade girls of all time, Joy, came in to computer class last term and told me that she was sad because her parents would not be coming for mid term break. Then she started to cry. I can't stand little girls crying: I have had sons, so I have developed immunity to boy tears, but I just can't handle girl tears very well. As we sat there, with me trying to think of something helpful to say, I started crying, which caused Joy to stop crying so she could comfort me.

2. Negative Encouragement: I think I am a natural encourager, but that gets old fast. So I told my sixth grade class that they would get a treat if they were able to master some database problems. Then I told them that I didn't want to spend money on THEM, I wanted to spend it on ME. So anytime they made a mistake, I praised them, and anytime they did something right, I yelled at them. I knew I was on to something when one kid bragged: `He yelled at me FOUR times today!'

3. Humiliation: For third graders, the only thing that works is to give them an opportunity to humiliate the teacher. I can't tell you why, but on a certain spreadsheet section I am doing with the third grade, I could get nowhere with them until I told them that for anyone who could do it perfectly. I would bunny hop around the class. Six minutes later, every kid had it right. In fact, I was forced to say something I never expected to say in my life when three kids asked for retroactive bunny hops:

Don't get greedy with bunny hops!

Nan went to a woman's retreat this weekend, so that left me alone with 10 boys. Here is what I learned:

I have grown in an important way: I know how to handle sick kids now.

When we were first here, when a kid came into the room and announce that he was going to get sick, I would jump up in a panic and yell `Not here! Go to the toilet!! NOT HERE!!!' Often the shock of being loudly instructed would result in an undesirable consequence.

On Friday night, a kid came into my room and announced that he was going to get sick. I realized my role is more like a hostage negotiator. I got up slowly from the bed and said in soothing tones `I am so sorry; where does it hurt?' as I gently but firmly guided him to the bathroom. As soon as he got into the bathroom, I HIT HIM IN THE KIDNEY AND SCREAMED `EMPTY IT RIGHT NOW!!' Besides the gentle wistfulness of the last sentence, I have realized that some discussions work better in bathrooms than bedrooms.

The drought has been ferocious in the last few months, and since Nan was gone, I met with some of the vegetable ladies. I asked one how her garden was, and she started crying. I always have been so glib, but Africa often leaves me with nothing to say. I patted her on the back, but I didn't know what to say. I've never been hungry, and my life doesn't hinge on whether my garden comes in. I just didn't know what to say. I didn't want to give empty words, but that is all I felt I had.

Your pal,

Steve

Even Aunt Nancy

There is always one event that signifies that yes, it is time for the end of the term. Our neighbor had college age twins visiting her, and we invited them over to do devotions with the guys. They are both bright cute woman, and after they sat down, one of the guys tooted loudly. And they all laughed loudly. And so I said loudly `That's it. In this dorm, we honor woman. We will never pass gas in front of a woman again, If you need to do business, excuse yourself and do it in another room. Never again in front of a woman. Is that clear?'

One of the guys very innocently asked `Even Aunt Nancy?' And at that point, I knew that it was time for the term break to begin. We are on three months and then the guys spend a month at home with their parents. I am going to help install Account Payables, build an ordering system for the library, deliver maize in the valley, and all sorts of other projects, but having the kids with their folks is a nice break.

There are things that catch you by surprise, even after nine months here. The butcher came by on Saturday, and I was the only one home, so I received our order. As I took the meat, I noticed how warm the package was, which was a surprise, since it was a cool day. And it struck me again: he has no electricity, and no refrigeration, so as soon as the animal is killed, they start to deliver the meat immediately. It cures me from ordering anything rare.

Someone gave us a subscription to Time magazine in July. We have received five copies of it to date. Magazines are routinely stolen, and sold on the streets. There was a guy here who subscribed to a woodworking magazine, and was driving into town and saw someone hawking the magazine. He bought it, and found his name on the back of the magazine. Another friend was sent candy from her fiancée, and there were tooth marks in it.

But it hit a new level last week. JT's grandfather sent him a check for his birthday, and the check was stolen and changed to be for $2800.00, quite a change from the $20.00 it began as. The bank caught it, and there won't be any charge to Papa, but imagine how you do business in a country where the mail is not secure. It is very very sad, and the government's response when confronted by a newspaper entailing the huge amount of stolen mail is `It could be a lot worse.'

You may have read about the bombing in Sudan. We have friends who work in the hospital there; the hospital is a target because it is a Christian hospital in an Islamic area, and for some reason, blowing up the only hospital in hundreds of miles staffed by volunteers is a neat idea. They are talking about evacuating the personnel, but the response of one of them has really stayed with me this week. A bomb went off less than 1000 yards from the hospital, and they suggested that the staff consider leaving. Almost to the person, the staff wants to stay and help, because they feel like if they leave, there will be no one there to help those people.

I read a quote this week about this kid who was killed in WWI. His journal was found, and it said `I will work, I will sacrifice, I will endure, I will fight cheerfully, and do my utmost, as if the issue of the whole struggle depended on me alone.'

I will never be a medical person in a war zone, but I want to live my life like they do. Whether I am in Kenya or Grapevine, Texas.

Your pal,

Steve

Feeding Dodging

Many of the children at the hospital have their mothers stay in the room with them. And African culture is much different than American culture in many ways, but perhaps in no way more different than breast-feeding.

My experience with many African women is that they think nothing of having a conversation with you, and in the midst of that conversation, drop their blouse and began feeding their child. And that is fine; I am grateful for the differences in cultures.

But I am not comfortable being in full view of a breast besides my brides, so it causes me to do two things:

- I can whip my head upwards so fast that I fear I will need to be treated for whiplash.

- When I approach an aisle and I notice that something new has emerged, I can change direction so rapidly that, especially if many women are feeding their children, I become something akin to a human pinball.

I call it Feeding Dodging, and I don't mind saying I'm getting pretty darn good at it.

Last year on our 14th wedding anniversary, I took Nan to the vending machine at the dorm we stayed at during orientation school and told her: `Honey, anything you want here, you can have.' We had meetings morning, noon and night, and we just had no opportunity to do anything else.

But on the 15th, you've got to do something special. And with the help of some friends who agreed to stay at our dorm all weekend, we got to go away to a very special place: the Mount Kenya Safari Club.

Normally, there is little chance that we could afford to go to a place like that. Prices are so high, and especially as a missionary, you don't usually have extra money. But because we are in Kenya for a year, we are legally residents, so we qualified for resident rates that are a sixth of the normal rate.

American actor William Holden founded the MKSC in 1959, and it is lovely, with beautiful gardens and wild forests, right at the foot of Mt Kenya. The views are just spectacular, with both mountain and forest views. Some friends that we went with are birders, and they saw 70 different kinds of birds.

MKSC has an animal orphanage, and we fed ostrich, monkeys, golden crested cranes, and bongos out of our hands. At one point, a monkey was leaning on Nan, and holding her hand to get more food. He later jumped on the 125-year-old tortoise named Speedy.

We were able to go to a park nearby for the afternoon and see elephants coming in to drink and bath, a chimp conservatory started by Jane Goodall, and pet the tame rhino.

A poacher orphaned this rhino when he was six months old, and he has lived around humans his whole life, so he is considered tame. To reach him, you walk several miles to the open space in which he lives, and suddenly you are standing in front of a 1.5 ton rhinoceros. He really seemed like a big dog; he ate out of our hands, and he let you pet him. And it was one of those experiences that you never expect to have in life.

A guard with a large rifle always attends him, because poachers are such a problem in Africa. As our guide told us: we shoot first, then ask questions. Rhinos and elephants have been decimated by poachers, and if the economy continues to deteriorate, many fear it will get worst.

I never expected to celebrate 15 years of marriage in Africa, but it will be an anniversary we will never forget. The secret of a happy marriage is to marry Nancy Peifer. Since she is already taken, I wish for you that you would experience all the joys of the covenant that I have. It has been a rich and wonderful 15 years.

Your pal,

Steve

Get Off the Gas, Get Off the Gas!!!

I was going to be different.

You know the stereotype; the nervous sweating driving instructor who frequently screams in panic and bursts into tears with seemingly no good reason.

Calm was my mantra, and I'm not ever sure what a mantra is. But I would gently reassure them and guide them into happy driving. After all, I had spent the term covering the curriculum with them and had fallen in love with all of them. It was going to be easy.

Not that driving here is easy. Kenya drives on the left, there are no automatics here, there are no paved roads, and we are in a very hilly area. But I was serene the night before; my bride was not, but I was.

The first driver did fine. She had driven in Nairobi with her father, and she was a very competent driver.

Then my problems began. The next driver stalled out 22 (no exaggeration) times. I thought that I might have to sit on her lap and operate the clutch for her. She came up with a different solution; she gave her full concentration to the pedals, at the exclusion of everything else. And she got it in gear. The car started moving, and she kept her eyes on her pride and joy, her feet.

In a calm voice, I said `It is good that you got the car in gear, but you must also steer the car.' Her reply will live with me the rest of my days: `Oh' said she as she continued to look at her feet while the left wheels of the car went up an embankment and stopped. She got out of the car, and I moved the car to a level area, but at this point I became aware that I was perspiring.

The next driver was what we driving instructors would call a nervous driver. She informed me that she could not drive, and had always fancied buses anyway. She stalled out the car several times. In a still gentle voice, I told her `Ease off the clutch and gently touch the gas pedal.'

Several things happen next. She put the car into gear, which was a good thing. But as she removed the clutch, she put the gas pedal all the way to the floor, which was a bad thing. She screamed rather loudly, and I said in a somewhat encouraging voice `Ease off the gas, but you got it into gear: Great job!' She then steered the car into an embankment with the gas pedal fully engaged, which was a worst thing. `Steer the car' I yelled in a somewhat panicked voice. `Where is the gas?' she screamed in a very panicked voice.

At this point, I was standing in my seat, pulling the emergency brake up as far as it would go, screaming as loud as I could: `**Get Off the Gas, Get Off the Gas!!!**' The car was confused: the gas pedal was fully engaged, as well as the brake. What did we actually want to do, I could imagine it asking us.

Finally it stopped, and as I tried to survey the damage, she asked `What is that smell?'

The answer was a sad one: `That used to be the brake.' But no damage to the car of any passengers, and we begin again next week....

We hired Charles to do a carving demonstration for our dorm boys. He makes his living carving wood into ornaments and spoons. He is an amazing guy; he had his thumb bitten off by a hyena that was attacking his cow. He fought it off, but lost his thumb and the use one finger in the battle. And somehow he has developed an incredible skill in carving.

He brought ten pieces of wood in various stages, to show the boys the process. Then he took a raw piece of olivewood, and began the work of making that into a serving spoon. His tools were a machete, a file, one piece of sandpaper, and a log. He made all the cuts with a machete, used the file and sandpaper to smooth out rough-cuts, and his log was his workbench, vise, and measuring tool.

In two hours, he turned the piece of wood into something beautiful. Without a thumb and with the crudest tools imaginable. The boys were just amazed, and again we hope for something that moves down to their hearts. Africa can break your heart, but it is full of people who have made something beautiful out of so little.

Your old pal,

Steve

Good Morning, Mrs. Peifer! My, What A Lovely Dress!

One of the great things about second term is you know more of what to expect, so it allows you, in the words of my English colleagues, the opportunity to be a little cheeky. I have trained this term of driving students to always greet Nancy, no matter what time it is and no matter what she is wearing, with the following phrase, best delivered in a halting monotone:

Good morning, Mrs. Peifer! My, what a lovely dress!

Mrs. Peifer is truly enjoying her greetings, and my shin should recover in a short while…

I had the opportunity to go into Nairobi to go to a computer show. The last show I went to in the states included entertainment by the rock group Chicago and the Pointer Sisters. This was a little different: it was in a mall, and there were 12 exhibitors. In every booth, there were power backups, because if you don't count on the power going off a dozen or so times a day, you are fooling yourself. I found about half of the people knowledgeable, and half full of wind, which is a higher ratio than the US. How hard it must be to run a computer company, with irregular power and horrible phone lines, but what an opportunity; India built a middle class in a generation by leapfrogging technology. Could it happen in Africa? I hope so.

JT turned 11 today, and it was a memorable birthday in lots of ways. Last year, his party was at Laser Quest; they shot each other with lasers. No laser quest in Africa, but lots of stars, so five of his buddies camped out last night. It gets cold here at night, and the winds were blowing strong, but when you are in fifth grade, camping out for the first time without the parents, the thrill is so great that you forget the cold, or probably closer to the truth, the cold is part of the thrill. They stayed up late talking about the adventures they are planning, and came in this morning cold, tired and exhilarated; a perfect birthday.

Grace's oldest son received his assignment for school. He is assigned to a boarding school, and the cost is about what the average African makes in a year. And there is so much graft and corruption at the school lever, that it put me in a foul mood: how can they justify this cost when no one can afford it, and why do they require uniforms that cost so much (answer: a prime minister owns the clothing outlet), and why do they require kids to buy books instead of lending the books like the states (answer: a politician owes the bookstore), and why do they destroy their children this way? And I was mad, as mad as I have ever been since I've been here.

But I got a powerful reminder of how unrelated things can work together. Grace's husband has been a non-provider for years; he was caught stealing by a previous employer, and he spends much of his time drinking and chasing woman. When they got the school bill, he disappeared for several days; this was not unusual for him.

What he was doing, however, was unusual for him. He was working. He was so shook up at the bill; he had found a five-day job. He didn't make much, but he was trying, and that is more than he has done in years. And it struck me: I came to Africa after my son died, but I am surprised that different things can work together in a pattern I can't see, but only marvel at.

Your pal,

Steve

How Do You Dismantle A Meat Loaf?

Email was down for the entire nation of Kenya this last 7 days. Kenya has only one satellite that handles all its email, and when it goes down, there is no plan B. When email goes down for an extended period, I start to imagine all sorts of wonderful news items I will receive:

- CUBS WIN WORLD SERIES
- DOW HITS 30000
- CURE FOR CANCER FOUND

Instead, what I received was a message from my good friend who is renting out house informing us that water is leaking from the downstairs bathroom and it will cost $1300 to repair and would I reply ASAP? Unfortunately, I received this message on Saturday and he sent it the previous Sunday. We are grateful for email, but in Kenya, it has its limitations.

We had cafeteria duty this week. Our job is to make sure that the smaller kids take some veggies, and drink some milk, and in general, don't waste food. Again, all the negotiations that I have done in my career have not prepared me for this:

Me: You need more than two peas.
Them: OK.
Me: You need more than THREE peas.
Them: How many?
Me: 25.
Them: How about eight?

This can go on a lot longer than you can imagine. I always lose.

But it doesn't come close to matching the case of the dismantled meatloaf. I walk by this kid, and there are thirty round balls of meat and three glasses of water on his tray.

Me: What is that?
Them: Meatloaf.
Me: Meatloaf?
Them: I hate the taste so I crush it into little balls and swallow them like pills. Wanna see?
Me: Excuse me...

We had a Kenyan preacher this morning who just returned from studies in Chicago. He told us that the church in Chicago offered its greetings: `Say hi to you guys!' He told a familiar story about the young boy at the seashore who was throwing starfish back into the ocean and the man said: `There are thousands of starfish on this beach. You can't throw enough back to make a difference.' And the kids looks at the guy and says `It makes a difference to this one.'

It really put things into perspective for me. I am so aware of my limitations, and the overpowering need here. And I can't come close to helping, or really understanding the cause of lots of the problem. But I feel like a senator from Illinois once said about trying to stop the destruction of the sand dunes in the state. He said, " When I was a young man, I wanted to save the world. When I was middle aged, I wanted to save the country. Now, as an old man, I just want to save the dunes."

There are three things I would like you to know about.

1. We work with an orphanage nearby. There can't be too many rougher blows in life than to be an orphan in Africa. You just wouldn't believe how they live. I can't change that, but I would like them to have a gift for Christmas. A perfect gift would be a Magna-Doodle. They are a kid's toy in the states that doesn't need batteries or much explanation. I would love to see the whole orphanage, each kid, get a Magna-Doodle.

2. We work with a Crippled Children's Hospital. In Africa, one of the saddest facts of life is children with problems are often hidden away, because they are an embarrassment to their families. Often, when they are brought in, something that would have been an easy procedure when they were infants turns into a big problem when they are older. The kids there play with rolled up rags. I would love there to be lots of crayons and coloring books and matchbox cars and children's books; nothing big, but so they would have something.

3. The famine continues. We would love to distribute more maize and beans in the valley. A 70 pound bag of maize costs about $30.00.

Lots of folks have asked if they could do anything for us. We really don't need anything, and we are grateful for all the support we have received.

But we would love to be able to give the kids with nothing something this Christmas. If you would like to send toys, would you send them to Steve Peifer AIM 135 Crooked Hill Road PO BOX 178 Pearl River, NY 10965? They will forward them to us in a way that will prevent items from being stolen. If you would like to donate to famine relief, you could send a check to Steve Peifer RVA PO Box 80, Kijabe, Kenya East Africa. Make the check payable to AIM Famine Relief and you will get a receipt that you can write off.

I hate to ask, and so early, but we expect more power outages and email problems, not less, and I wanted to let you know so you might have time to do something if you wanted to.

Please note: When I was in the States, I got 2 billion requests like this everyday. It won't hurt my feelings if you are already giving and don't want to hear any more requests. But I thought you would want to know.

Your old pal,

Steve

Your Pal, Steve

How Would You Like Your Zebra Cooked?

Remember the end of July when you were a kid? All the sudden it would hit you; summer is almost over and I haven't finished my fort, or had the big water balloon fight, and I haven't slept outside hardly at all and there was such a rush to get it all done.

The adult version of that occurred this week at RVA. The kids arrive back on Monday, and once they do, it is 24x7 for three months, so the week before classes begin is pretty frantic with everyone taking their final flings. And we were no exception: we tried to put 15 pounds of lard in a ten-pound bag.

Tuesday was the biggest contrast day we've had since we've been in Africa. We were invited to Grace's house for lunch. It took us an hour walking to get there, and it was lots of uphill climbing. I think it was Matthew who said `Dad, she does this everyday!'

Her house has a breath taking view. It is a very small home, but it did have two windows, which is a great luxury here, and they had a poured cement floor, which is very rare. We had brought a Nerf football, and we had lots of fun throwing it around; none of them had ever thrown an American football, so the styles of throwing varied greatly.

We had a wonderful meal (included was a mixture of potato and beans which was green due to the pumpkin leaf flavoring) and after the meal, as is Kenyan tradition, we played games. After several games, they sang and danced for us. And then, for perhaps the only time on earth, the Peifer family was asked if `Perhaps you have a song to sing for us?'

It needs to be said: we are not the von Trapps. Or anything close. I was kicked out of the choir at a church because I could make a whole section go flat. But we stumbled through a song and were received graciously, but there was no call for an encore.

After we got home, we cleaned up and went, with 5 carloads of other folks to Nairobi for a farewell dinner at the Inter-Continental Hotel. This is the fancy hotel in Kenya, and with crisp linens and a pianist playing in the background. it didn't seem like Africa. We were saying goodbye to a couple whom had worked here for 20 years, and for a fine meal for both Nan and I, with extra thrown in for tip and to help pay for the retiring couple, it cost me $11.00. But both fancy hotels and concrete slabs are Africa; we don't often get to live in both worlds in the same day.

The ride home was thrilling also. There are very very few lampposts in Africa, and many many Africans believe that using headlights wears down the battery, so every night drive is an adventure. We made it back safely, but night driving is not for the faint of heart.

The next day we climbed Mt. Longonot. We can see it from our window, and although it is not a huge mountain, it was plenty steep for me. As we began to climb, we passed by a herd of zebra not 20 feet away. It was a tough climb, but I had one of the most wonderful experiences I've had as a father. Every father has the hope that their children will go beyond what they have accomplished, and we got a graphic view of it, as our boys were 20 minutes ahead of us, and we could see them forging ahead.

We finally got to the top, and ate our lunch and looked into the crater (Longonot was once a live volcano) JT and Matthew then proceeded to run down (it was three hours up and 2 hours down). I did not run; if fact, I was reminded of those T-shirts I have seen which say `I climbed Mt Longonot'. I am going to market one that says `I fell off.'

Friends invited us out to dinner on Thursday, and we had a vivid example that we were in Africa. They had zebra on the menu, and several ordered it. We all laughed when the waiter asked `How would you like your zebra cooked?' It was very tasty, but I'm afraid I still don't know the answer to the question.

Your pal,

Steve

I Am Not A Toilet

This time I was determined.

During the break, we have the opportunity to take Swahili again. Since I had made a fool of myself on the last one, I was determined not to make my instructor laugh.

Which is tough to do. In general, Kenyans are a very polite folk, and would think it would be the height of rudeness to laugh at an inept, earnest American. Last term I managed to make them laugh quite often, but this was this term, and it was going to be different.

I did ok the first two days, but on the third day, we had to speak in the negative tense. I had to say `I am not something' and I was so thrilled that I understood which tense to use that I realized that I didn't know what I wasn't. So I improvised.

The teacher looked at me with a shocked expression, and then held his hand to his face. At this point, I knew I was in trouble. When someone is determined not to laugh and loses it, he loses it big time. Between gales of laughter, he said `You just said you are not a toilet!' Then he tried to regain composure, and then loudly said `YOU SAID YOU ARE NOT A TOILET!!'

We broke for chai, and I went to run an errand. When I stepped into the break room, he looked at me and then broke down again, and told his wife, who was the other instructor, `HE SAID HE IS NOT A TOILET!'

It was a long week in Swahili class, but the instructor called me a mzee, which is an elder, and prefaced it with `This is an insult to white people, but Africans like to be called elders; it means that we are beginning to be respected.' So when I return to the states and I get lip about how old I am, will I have a retort.

We went to the hospital today, and saw the usual sad cases. So much of this year has been hard. We have seen the most brutal things in Africa. There is so much poverty, so much illness, so much desperation. When you leave the country for a year, you find out who your friends are, but more, you find out who aren't, and that is a hard thing to see. The economic cost has been great, and you have so many goals you realize you won't achieve in your last few months.

But a little boy in the hospital just couldn't stop grinning at the truck you gave him, and his father's eyes filled with tears. A little girl got her first baby doll, and promised me she would take very very good care of her.

As we left the hospital, Matthew told me `Dad, I know its crazy, but every time I go to the hospital and play with those kids, I feel like I'm changing the whole world.'

It's been a tough year, but it has been worth it all.

Your pal,

Steve

I Do Better When I Don't Know Nothing

I need to confess the real reason I came to Africa.

I just didn't want to hear `The Heart Will Go On' ever again. I am convinced that the reason for road rage in the United States was people hearing that song and deciding that violence was the only alternative.

You can imagine my joy for the past two weeks as I passed the music building and strains of that song reverberated through the cement. That song is annoying with professional production: imagine sixth graders playing it.

Well, tonight they did play it at the music concert. And they didn't play the song. They grabbed it, wrestled it to the floor and gnawed on it like a piece of raw meat. Nan says I am overreacting and that it was cute, but she isn't the driving teacher.

I have so many surreal moments in Africa I am always surprised that I don't wake up in America and loudly proclaim `Never anchovies and onions before bed again!' This week's was due to our good friend and neighbor back home who managed to get some of our CD's out here in the last shipment of toys. We only brought 24 CDs out, and you can't quite imagine how sick we are of all of them. He managed to get a dozen of them in one of the boxes.

On Wednesday nights and Saturday mornings, the entire dorm eats here. Nan is in charge to supervising cooking, and I am in charge of clean up. One of the CDs was an Alan Jackson CD, and he is a country singer in the states with a song called `Gone Country.' This week, while we were washing dishes, we put on that CD, and all the Korean guys sang along with the refrain:

> Gone country
> Look at them boots
> Gone country
> New kinda' look
> Gone Country!!!

Listening to 4 Koreans sing Gone Country at the top of their lungs in Africa is one of those surreal moments.

But as we speak, another surreal moment is occurring. We are watching the Super Bowl tape tonight, and there is something really odd watching it in March. Besides the time factor, all the adults here have been putting their predictions in the pool for the NCAA.

You have to understand I love the NCAA with all my heart. Every year in the states, I read everything I can on it, watch as many of the games that I can, and place my predictions in with great confidence.

And lose in the first round. This year, as I made my predictions for the pool, I realized I had not seen one game or read one article about the NCAA. It did not stop me from being passionate about my picks, nor did it stop anyone else from loudly disagreeing with everyone else. And no one here has seen a game this season. It is a guy thing, perhaps the ultimate guy thing.

Perhaps the most humiliating thing to occur to me is that I am currently ranked second (against 44 others) in my predictions of the NCAA. I do better when I don't know nothing, which probably could be a song for Alan Jackson someday.

Speaking of basketball, the season ended and I was undefeated against the other three coaches here at RVA. Because of that, we got to pick an all star team and play against two other schools. The first team came for it, and several members of their 7th grade squad appeared to be in the need for a shave. It looked like several came holding car keys, and the game was not pretty: we lost 29-6. And I tried everything, and every combination of players, but they were just too much for us.

But we got another opportunity on Wednesday. I am the only coach who has both boys and girls on his team because 1. I believe in equal opportunity and 2. Sixth grade girls are a foot taller than sixth grade boys. We started the game, and while the other team still had the height advantage, we were playing great. We were playing so great that at the half, we were winning 20-0 and I had played every player.

The second half was the antithesis of what a coach should do. I thought: he can't dribble, she can't pass and he won't shoot; put them in together. And they would dribble, pass and score. I looked like I was running the score on them, and started saying things like `Let's that it easy out there!' I groaned when we rebounded, and when the other team finally scored, I yelled the loudest. We won 35-2, and I am retiring. It won't get any better.

I have taught a Sunday school this term for 8th and 9th graders, and it has been a challenge to me. It is somehow comforting that even teens in Africa grow sullen and self absorbed. How do you reach past that has been my question, and I haven't had a good answer.

But today, on the last Sunday school of the term, I brought them down to the hospital. There are several children with hydro-cephaly, which is an illness that can cause a baby's head to be three times its normal size. It is one of the hardest things to look at that I have seen since I have been here in Africa. The week before we went, I told the class to read this Scripture:

>Seek first the Kingdom of God
>And the wealth of His righteousness
>For wherever your treasure lies
>There will you find your heart.

My class played well with the children, and enjoyed the experience. Two of them were crying at the end, and when I asked why, one of them said `I think I found my heart.'

There are good tears, you know.

Your pal,

Steve

I Love the Cowboys Dallas!

It was time. My seven days of Swahili had prepared me to go to the Masai Market. What is it, you ask? Imagine as you exit a major expressway, you begin to see dozens of people walking rather precariously above the traffic to a market of hundreds of Africans spreading their goods for sale on the dirt ground. And you have a target on your forehead: Inside the bull's-eye reads: Here lies a dumb rich white person: charge as much as you can.

Your mission? Bargain. It's an art form in Kenya, and anyone who pays full price is the same as the one who pays full price for a car in the states. The car analogy is an apt one: this is a land of car salespeople. Anything to make a connection. JT was wearing a Dallas Cowboys shirt and at least a dozen men loudly proclaimed: `I love the Cowboys Dallas!' I saw one gentleman wearing a U of Chicago sweatshirt and told him I attended a class there. He told me he had also, and pointed to the date on the shirt: 1892. One guy told me that it was a bad omen if I didn't buy; I told him I didn't believe in omens. He then loudly proclaimed `I am again borned.' Whatever you wanted to hear, it would be said.

I saw a batik I liked; it is dye on cloth, and it is quite the art form here. `Steve' (there were about 20 `Steve's' that day) responded to my question `Ni shillingi ngapi?' (How much) with 10 thousand shillings. I grabbed my heart and moaned `Ni ghani Sana' (It is very expensive). He protested about the integrity of his artistic vision … or that he was going to eat bratwurst for lunch. I told him that his price was so high that I would suffer a heart attack, fall down by hill, and be hit by a car. Anyway, this went on and on and it finally got down to 700 shillings. What a day!

A few special moments:

- Matthew comes in and calmly informs me that there is a large male baboon in the outside trash.

- To celebrate the end of language school, they announce a goat roast. It tastes good, and rather like you might expect goat to taste.

- I have read the Wall Street Journal since I was 19. I inquire what it will cost to get a subscription in Kenya. I am informed that a one-year subscription will cost $2,700 dollars and it will arrive 5-7 days later. I decide to remain uninformed.

- Fred and I are sitting discussing the day. It is a chance for me to work on my Swahili and to know a national better; for him, it is an opportunity to him to laugh at my accent and pronunciation. At one point in the conversation, Fred tells me that he is hoping to save up to buy concrete, because his home has dirt floor, and windows, because the cardboard is a invitation for thieves. Fred is considered wealthy by African standards, and again I do not know what to say.

A friend writes to me about his struggles at the university he has labored in for years. He is a smart, working charismatic individual who has given his whole life to this institution which is now treating him badly. And he feels bad complaining about his life. But if anything has become clear in the last month, it is every life is important, and that we all struggle against the circumstances we are in, and one is not higher or greater than the other. My hope is that these notes give a picture of what is here, but not to lessen what our family and friends struggle with. OK?

Your old pal,

Steve

I Never Saw THAT at the Fort Worth Zoo

We had the opportunity to go to another game park this week. Samburu is known for the river that runs through the park. It was completely dry. You could walk across it. Which is why there was a staff member whose job was to walk back and forth all night to make sure that none of the leopards came across to the people side. Whenever you think you have a bad job, remember, you could be walking back and forth with a flashlight making sure leopards don't eat the guests.

I am not sure how to say the next thing except to say that when animals are out in the wild, you see things you don't see at the Ft. Worth Zoo. Elephants and zebras leave nothing to the imagination. It leads to interesting discussions in the car with young children.

But a visit to a game park is a great opportunity to marvel at the wonder of creation, and I did marvel at it until... our truck got stuck, and I got to go out and push.

Pushing a car is always fun, but pushing in a game park ten minutes after you saw a leopard leap from a tree is an all together different experience. After many minutes, we got the car out, and one of the rangers came by and hollered at us for being out of the car. When I asked him about the leopards, he said `They only kill at night! But the buffalo were starting to snort!' As I looked up, I saw many buffalo looking at me with anger in their eyes, and recalled stories of buffaloes attacking Range Rovers and winning, and gladly got into the car and longed for a little less marvel.

Later in the week, we went to Nairobi for a few days. It was unsettling in many ways. We went bowling in a very modern 12 lane alley, complete with automatic scoring, the only one in Nairobi. And the only people bowling were Indians and whites. We did not see an African bowling the whole time. It is time for the kids to start reminding them of life in the States, but I left there feeling, for the first time since I have been in Africa, ashamed of myself for what I had done.

Later we saw a movie, the first we have seen since we have been in Africa. Playing at the theater were The Matrix, You've Got Mail, and the one we saw, Toy Story2. Before a movie is shown, there is a government newsreel that is so bad it is quite amusing. It consisted of the President watching the military march in several different arenas, each time to `the thrill of the spectators.' Spin city is not an art form yet in Kenya.

On Sunday, we went with Grace to her church. We got to ride the legendary matatus, which is a minivan that is crammed to the gills with people. We were in a Nissan mini van, probably 15 years old. And we managed to get 18 people in it. I was in the front seat with Matthew on my lap, someone sitting over the gearshift and the driver. Nan and JT were somewhere in the back. Grace told us later that it was a very comfortable ride.

The church was metal sidings and cement floors with benches with no back. We got there at 10 and it lasted until 2. We were the only white people there, and the two kids in front of me were so fascinated by me that they turned around in their seats and looked at me the whole time. This did not help me enter into the spirit of worship, and I probably didn't help matters by making faces at them to make them giggle, which led to lots of kids coming over so I would make a face at them, which I am sure the pastor truly appreciated.

Afterwards, we were invited to lunch in the back of the church with the pastor, who apologized that we would have to eat with our hands because the church could not afford knifes and forks. The boys were thrilled, but it was humbling and disconcerting for Nan and I.

We walked a mile back to get on the matatu, and then we realized that we had an easy ride before. We got on, and waited. Matatus don't go until they are full, and full is a relative term. While we were waiting, there was an older man in front of us who was very ill, and he was going to the hospital, but that did not speed things up. We waited until they got 30 people on this minivan. Kids were on laps, and we put seven people to a bench. The last four people were pushed in the van, and when the screams of the passengers indicated that they were closing the door on people, the solution was to not close the side door, so four people grabbed on for dear life as we left.

Nan and I couldn't tell if we smelled transmission fluid or brake fluid, but after we went for a short time, we stopped and let two people off. Incredibly, four more got on and we got to our destination. As I got off, it struck me: this is transportation for most of the people of Kenya. That or walking.

I've complained about my commute in Dallas before, with air conditioning and a comfortable chair and a great sound system. Slap me if I ever complain about it again.

Your pal,

Steve

I Wish My Skin Was Black

Every evening we have devotions in the dorm. Our tradition is to invite different people in the community to come and share; where else could you have people do something like that? Last week, one of the single women came and brought a video that she made when she bungee jumped in Victoria Falls, Africa. The video was dramatic, and she gave a wonderful talk about trust and faith.

What did fifth grade boys get out of the talk? The next morning, three different guys had tied their socks together, tied one end off the top bunk, and the other end around their ankles, trying to see what it felt like to bungee jump. I can't answer what it felt like, but I have many unkind opinions of what it was like to untie used socks...

On Friday night, Matthew went with a friend to spend the night. Our eight year old walked a mile in the dark with another eight year old to his home, something I cannot imagine in the states but didn't worry about here, in this part of Africa. They spent the day together, and had fun swimming and playing.

Matthew came home sunburned, and wondered if Josh had gotten sunburned. We replied that probably not, because Josh is a Kenyan with dark skin. His reply was classic Matthew:

"I wish MY skin was black".

With the help of some other friends, we were able to help Grace cover the tuition for her oldest son. But the educational system in this country is so corrupt that when the government announced that they would reduce school fees in half, the schools simply ignored the government, and kept fees the same level.

The final blow came when we got all the money together, which is about twice what the average African makes in a year. It couldn't be paid in cash; it had to be in a money order. And there are some good reasons for that, considering all the thieves in the schools. (In the schools defense, many of the teachers have not been paid in 5 months) So it had to be a money order.

And the money order cost three weeks wages.

I have never understood revolutions before I came to Africa, and I think if there is unrest here, the poor will be the most hurt, but at what point do you throw up your hands and say `Enough is enough' and trash a system that robs and steals from its own people?

I don't know the answer to the question, but I understand the question now.

Your pal,

Steve

Letters from 2001

You Are One Of Us
— October 7, 2001

You know how in the US everyone will ask you how you are and you say fine? And how that gets old? In Kenya, people greet you with Habari yako which means how are you and you respond Mzuri sana which means fine.

I've tried to change it with inflection. I say Habari in a normal voice and then, on the last syllable of yako I sound like my underwear just bunched up. It never fails to get a response from Kenyans. But in the spirit of trying to learn a new word a day, I have begun answering Baridi sana. Translated: I am very cool.

If you are a lover of irony, Kenyans try to correct me every time I say this. 'No, it is very warm.' The irony part is: I have never been cool one day in my life. So it falls on me to try to explain what cool is. I think you can make a case that Africa invented cool; they just don't know what it means. Having me explain cool is one of the great reasons that they need MORE missionaries in Africa, preferably some cool ones.

We went to Mahi Maihu this weekend. Researchers have traced the spread of AIDS in Africa to truck stops throughout the country. Mahi Maihu is a truck stop community absolutely devastated by AIDS. There are hundreds of orphans in this little town, so we went down to deliver food and play with orphans.

Before we went to play with the kids, we brought some food and clothes for some widows in the area. Suburban America cannot prepare you for this level of poverty. One woman lived in a home that was roughly the size of two cubicles. She had dirt floors, mud walls and two very crude chairs. It was there that she and her six children lived. None of them had shoes, and all the clothing was donated hand me downs.

She told us that she managed to get her children fed, although milk is a luxury item that only the wealthy enjoy in Kenya. Feeding them means one meal of rice and maize a day, and this is served without plates, knives or forks; they grab handfuls of it and eat it standing up.

Her concern is school fees. (There is no free education in Kenya, so parents must pay for their children to be educated. I have been at a school in Kenya where a child whose parents could not afford school fees snuck into the class and was beaten with a stick for returning without paying.) She could afford to feed them one meal, but school fees were beyond her, and she knew that without education, her children would never have much of an opportunity in life. To live in that kind of poverty must be overwhelming; to know that your children will also live like that must be one of the most painful things one could endure.

The woman at the orphanage cooked a huge meal of stew over an open fire. Kenyan woman are used to being around open flames; they can handle the heat. I would ask if the fifty-pound pots were hot as I grabbed them to load into a van. They assured me that they were not; I can assure you that they were so hot that it was all I could do to not drop the pans and risk orphans not getting their meal. They thought that I had white hands; all I can say is, someday I will have them over for some Mexican food, and we will see who can handle the heat.

I was honored to be remembered at the orphanage because of many of you. The last time I was there we were able to deliver hundreds of toys to the children, and many of them remembered and greeted me. Some ran to get their Magna Doodles and show me their latest drawings. Although English is their second language, I did manage to teach a group of 50 kids to shout `I love Texas' at the tops of their lungs, which I'm sure was very educational for them. Without words, I managed to lose in six races, have a hopping contest, a hold your breath contest, and a you-can't-smile contest.

The director showed me the dorms. I hope to return to take some pictures, but these little children live in tough circumstances. The big problem they have is many of the children wet their beds, and that causes the foam mattresses to smell awful. There are 18-24 children in a room, and sometimes the odor was more than I could bear. Some of the mattresses are over five years old; there is just no money to buy new ones. The dining hall is in real need of new tables, because they have so many children and the tables are so old that they are breaking down. It means that many of these kids stand when they eat. We've tried to repair them, but the wood is rotting and it is just time for new ones.

As we were leaving, many of the children were clinging to us. The employees of the orphanage work so hard, but there are so few of them and so many children. Children need adult attention, and they get so little of it.

I was crying, and the director grabbed my hands and looked me in the eyes: `You are one of us.'

It's the nicest thing anyone has said to me since I've been in Kenya.

Your pal,

Steve

Wood Surfing
— *October 21, 2001*

Some people like to be at the forefront of a trend. Since this is scientifically impossible for me, I am more inclined to celebrate the end of a trend. In the states, there was a radio ad playing right before we returned to Africa in which a young child earnestly yelled `Ovaltine rocks!' I think it is safe to say that the expression `That rocks' has passed out of cool.

In the same spirit, I wish to announce the end of the goatee. I started growing one last week. Since it has come in Santa white, it has already solicited kindly remarks like `it makes you look even older' which I'm sure will be the death knoll for that look.

A few weeks before we came out to Africa, someone called us and asked if we wanted to be on his container of items going to Africa. He was shipping a container by boat, and it was 90% full, and he wanted to fill it up. Until that point, we hadn't considered doing one, but that made the price affordable.

The biggest thing we wanted to ship was our mattresses. You can't buy a real mattress in Kenya; you can get a foam pad, and that is fine for young Turks, but not for someone with a white beard. What we discovered is ten percent of a container is a lot; we were able to get lots and lots of stuff on it. We had kind friends who helped us pack and drove down a truck to Houston where it shipped out to go by boat to Africa.

We received an email that the container had arrived, and that we should be there for the opening. I went into town and we arrived at the yard. Hundreds of containers, as large as a rail car, spread out for several miles. It was a two-mile walk just to get to our container.

The procedure is: your shipping company has the lock. You go there to unlock and witness customs inspecting the container, to make sure nothing gets stolen. And we were ready to do it, except that when we opened the container, there was a large piece of lumber that sealed the container.

The Kenyans limited tools were no match for the machine driven nails. After an hour, there was no real progress. I took a crow bar and pried the top enough to get a handgrip, and I pulled myself up to the top and stood on the plywood, hoping my weight would cause it to buckle. After several minutes, two Kenyan men jumped up there with me.

It became evident that it would work, but it would take some time. What does one do when you are in the middle of a shipping yard in Kenya, standing with two other men trying to break down plywood?

In an odd way, it sort of seemed like surfing. Because I was in Kenya and wanted to be culturally sensitive, I knew I had to sing the perfect surfing song:

Surfing Safari

Since I have been back in Kenya, teaching two non-English speaking Africans to sing the refrain `Surfing Safari, yeah Surfing Safari' while standing atop of a huge container must be the most surreal moment to date. After about ten minutes and two `Sing again' the wood finally gave and we were able to get into the container.

We then hauled out about twenty pieces of the container. Almost 40 different people came by to look, to ask questions, or most likely, to hope to hear more singing. After almost three hours, we were told to return the pieces to the container.

While we were waiting, I spent some time with a young man named Moses. He is a newlywed, and makes a fair living, but lives in one of the worst slums in Kenya. It has almost one million people in it according to some estimates, and I am going to visit him in December when school is out if we have a vehicle. I asked him why he lived there.

Kenyans revere family life. Because he is the eldest son, it is his duty to help his younger brothers and sisters get educated. Because he was educating his younger brother, he could not afford any housing except the slum. I've driven by that place, and it is truly horrible. To choose to live there to help your brother is one of the most remarkable sacrifices I know of.

They delivered everything to our home on Friday. Everything, that is, but the mattresses. We don't know if they are on a container, or someone is having a very good night sleep that shouldn't, but it is one of the wonders of being in Kenya.

The one thing that arrived was our music. We brought over lots of CDs this time. I've told all my Kenyan friends: I will learn your customs and attempt to learn your language, but by the time I am done with you, you will know Motown well. By the time I leave Kenya, I have high expectations that all my Kenyan friends will know the difference between Martha Reeves and the Vandells and Junior Walker and the All Stars.

It's the least I could do.

Your pal,

Steve

Your Pal, Steve

Habari Zenu?

— October 27, 2001

Habari zenu? Which is Swahili for "How are y'all?" We are fine — at least as fine as world circumstances currently allow. I've been meaning to sit down and write an update from my (Nancy's) perspective. With all that has transpired since 9/11 I've been hesitant to write of more ordinary things, but the ordinary does continue in the midst of the greater picture.

Many of you have asked about our good friend Grace. Yes, she is again working for us and helping us out with cooking & cleaning so we can do all the things that RVA has asked us to do. It has been wonderful to reconnect with her and get caught up on our year apart. Because Fred has been hired by the school, we have a new young man helping us with our extensive yard here at Twiga Dorm. Many of you will remember when I wrote of walking home from my friend Florence's house the last time we were here. It is a 7-kilometer walk and it is not all flat_ Her son Joel walked most of the way home to show me the way and to protect me. He graciously took a lot of ridicule from Kenyans wondering why he was walking with a white woman At that time he had finished secondary school-quite an accomplishment here in Kenya-but he was unable to find any work. As we returned we were thrilled to be able to hire him to work for us! (Florence was thrilled too!) He's a great guy and we are enjoying getting to know him.

Let me tell you a bit about our new home. It is attached to a dorm, but is much more a separate house than our previous dorm since our dorm guys are junior high-ers who need less hands-on attention. It has an incredible view of the valley. After 5 weeks the view can still stop me dead in my tracks. In design it is a bit like a ski lodge in Colorado with huge windows all across the front. We love that part of it. The rest is a bit rustic. It is wood paneled in the living room and has wooden floors in about half of the house. Those wooden floors are so old and have such big cracks between the boards that when you sweep, by the time you get to the other side most of the dirt is gone having sifted down between the boards! I guess that's a nifty self-cleaning device. Where it is not wood paneling it is cement-walls and floors with copious cracks for character. The kitchen has character, which is another way of saying it is very unique! But for the most part, and since we have ousted most of the roach community that inhabited prior to our arrival, I like it.

The bathroom also has character, an aged character. The counter-top (which I am grateful for!) is a floral Formica such as I have never seen before. The sink and tub are blue matte (not gloss and not matte by origin). The toilet is white and only fully flushes solid waste about once every 15 flushes.

But it is home and we are feeling at home in it. We are together here for three meals a day and I'll trade my gleaming chrome and shiny porcelain for that any day. God has been so good to us. We laid aside some things (but they were just things) and He has blessed us with that which is more valuable.

Last week I went to visit my best friend here in Kenya. Her name is Olive and she is a college educated single woman of 35. She is highly respected in this community and in an even larger area of Kenya's Africa Inland Church community. She works mornings in the RVA high school library and afternoons in the elementary library with me.

She invited me to her home on Wednesday. It's about a 15-minute walk from RVA campus. On the way a rat ran across our feet. Her house is perched on the side of a hill too. She rents it from the family that lives just up the hill from her. Her "house" is an 8'x 8' room attached to 2 other same-sized rooms. It has no electricity; she uses a kerosene lantern at night. There is no running water. She cooks over a single gas eye stove-no oven. Her bathroom is outside and up the hill. In her room she has a single bed, small sofa, one chair, 2 cupboards and one small shelf. That's all. One of her neighbors is a doctor. He lives in a similar 8' x 8' sized room. She loves her house. As she says, "I live a simple life. And I am very happy. God has blessed me."

We do miss all of you and think of you often. And we would love to hear what you did last Wednesday!

Love, Nancy

Towel Bingo
— *October 29, 2001*

We're like the old joke: guy goes to Vegas in a $50,000 car and returns home in a $300,000 bus. We had a four bedroom, 2.5 bathroom home in Texas; now we have six showers and four toilets in the dorm.

J.T., Matthew, Nan and I all share a bathroom, and that is fine; we know it is a luxury to have running water. We build a fire if we want hot showers, and it has been cozy except for one thing.

Our boys will dry themselves on whatever is available. The thought that this might not be your towel has never crossed their minds; in fact, I am convinced that if the Magna Charta was in our bathroom, they would dry with that. All that leads to interesting times when you get out of the shower; did they get my towel today? I'm afraid I am not doing well in towel bingo.

It is so easy to get so busy here that you can forget the extraordinary things some of the students have gone through. People from the American Embassy were on campus this week because there were death threats against the parents of two of the children here. Their parents are working in a Muslim area, and there are people very unhappy with them. The kids were so shook up, and it wasn't safe for them to go to be with their parents, so they had a couple of very scary days. The parents believe that if they leave at the first sign of trouble, they will be sending the wrong message, so they are staying. I admire their courage and conviction, and I pray for their kids.

Some of my students have seen so much in their short lives. One of my students was camping, and a horde of rhinos charged her tent. They were able to get on top of a car and stay there until morning. More than a dozen have been evacuated from the areas they were serving; one kid had thirty minutes to leave before there was a slaughter in their compound. One girl talked about her friend being murdered, but first her friend had to witness her own mother and father being killed before her eyes.

It so grieves me that children have to know the horrors of war, and it especially hurts me that it is happening in the United States. I still can't comprehend all that has happened in America, but even over here, we feel violated for what has happened to the USA. Kenya doesn't let you forget you are an American either; there is an anti American march every Friday in Nairobi. Although many Kenyans are supportive to the US, many Muslims in Kenyan are very anti American.

Last week, they had a special night for the little kids. The seniors would be big brothers and big sisters to the little ones. Kenyan seniors were big brothers for American little kids, and vice versa. One of the little Kenyan kids dressed up like a Masai warrior, wearing a blanket draped over his shoulders and little else, When his white big brother saw how he was dressed, he ran home and came back dressed like a Masai also.

It's one of the reasons I love this place.

Your pal,

Steve Peifer

Where Is The Most Embarrassing Place You Have Ever Had An Itch?
— *November 4, 2001*

Make no mistake about it: the person who will get the largest crown in heaven is the woman who teaches the combined first and second grade class. I get them for 45 minutes a week, and in the computer class they range from `I'm afraid of mice' to `Can't we upgrade the operating system?' I don't know how she does it, and I am so glad I am not her I don't quite have words. It is the longest 45 minutes of the week.

Her class puts out a little newspaper every month, and I was interviewed this week by the class. These are actual questions:

> THEM: Where is the most embarrassing place you have ever had an itch?
>
> ME: I will get back to you.
>
> THEM: Have you ever gotten really mad at your sister because she ate the last four cookies and you only got one?
>
> ME: I'm not sure.
>
> THEM: What is your third favorite thing to drink?
>
> ME: Ummmm

The line of questioning continued for longer than I thought possible.

Returning to Africa has offered one surprise: I am not as surprised by what gave me the shakes three years ago. I can go into the hospital and see the most horrible deformities and not react to them anymore. I never understood how doctors could do it, but I understand it now. You can get used to anything. I don't want to get jaded or uncaring, but I don't think that is what is going on. To be effective, you've got to move past the shock, and I think I'm past it now. When I was here before, I would leave a room and get sick after I'd seen some of the kids I've seen. I can go to the worst cases and hold them now, and I'm grateful for it. I'm just surprised.

The hardest part of being away is when something serious happens to family or friends back home. One of our best friends had serious surgery last week, and we couldn't do anything for her. It's a helpless feeling, and I hope that hurt never goes away. It's a way of feeling attached.

Your pal,

Steve

Your Pal, Steve

Bureaucratic Safari
— *November 11, 2001*

How did I come to listen to Korean Rap? Well, aren't you supposed to get involved with the interests of your children? One of my dorm kids LOVES Korean rap, so it came to me to ask him` Hey, can I groove on your jam?' Or something to that effect. So, I listened to a CD of Korean Rap. I actually love American rap, especially when I can't make out the words. I love the energy. It's just when I can make out the words that I am depressed and horrified. Not knowing the words was actually helpful, and now I can say I have become exposed to a new music form. Which is not exactly the kind of art form that I expected to be exposed to when I moved to Kenya.

We had to do our alien registration this week. Although you have to have a passport to come into Kenya, and you pay no small fee in order to stay in Kenya, one must also be registered as an alien. It seems like it would be a fast and easy process, but it wasn't.

You just don't go to Nairobi and register. You have to go to Nairobi (one hour each way) and fill out some paperwork. You also pay your fee. This enables you to return the following week to actually begin the process. Why it can't be done the same day is a question without an answer, for they do no work during the week.

We arrive when the offices opened at 8:30am. There were four windows, none of which were labeled. We stood in one line for a period of time, while people in the back stared at us. Finally, one of them collected paperwork of people who had appointments for this week. That person disappeared for 45 minutes. When I looked in the back, there were files everywhere; on the floor, in the chairs, in no order that I could see.

We sat and waited. Finally, they started to call names. After another thirty minutes, our name was called. There wasn't a line; it was just a group of people hovering around a window. The woman behind the counter looked at our forms, and asked us to sign our names. At one point, she said `chai' a common drink that is also a euphemism for a bribe. But they didn't know whom they were dealing with because:

1. I can't pay a bribe; I'm a missionary.
2. I've negotiated contracts worth millions of dollars.
3. No one can more naturally play dumb better than me. I kept saying I wasn't thirsty, so after 20 minutes, we were given the forms back and told to go to another room to get finger printed.

I've never been finger printed before, but I don't that it is like this anywhere else. They took all my fingers, and then a handprint of each hand. Afterwards, they pointed to a pile of yarn and told us that we could wipe our hands on that. As we were doing so, they told us that we could return in a month to actually pick up our form. We left after about three hours there.

The sad part of this is that Kenya doesn't understand what this costs them. I'm certainly not vital to Kenya, but taking up this much time eats up opportunities to help orphans and sick kids in the hospital. I saw a doctor there who had been there as long as we had, and all I could think of is how many people wouldn't see him so he could wait in a line to get a sheet of paper.

Kenya has started to not allow short term doctors to practice medicine in our area. The hospital near us attracts surgeons who come at their own expense for short periods and do extensive amounts of surgeries in their specialties. It allows us to find kids with special problems and let them know when a surgeon with that skill is coming. Then they are operated on for free.

Kenya is now saying that if you don't come for a year, you can't use your medical skills. What is the point of this? To encourage doctors to stay longer? I'm amazed at how many doctors find time and money to come as it is; this will not help the situation. It will make it worse, far worse. Spending several hours of my life in a pointless line is one thing; preventing doctors from helping needy children is quite another. But they are both borne of the same thing: a government that no longer thinks of anything it does or any of its consequences; it just does it because it can. It is so ridiculous, and in the end, the banality of evil is what exhausts one. You can battle against an evil terrorist; how do you fight against an underpaid clerk following stupid orders?

I think I understand why people give up. I never had to fight city hall in the states, but I have a greater empathy for those who do.

We went to New Life Home on Sunday. It is an orphanage for abandoned infants. One child was actually put down a latrine and somehow survived for several days. By the time she was found, ants had actually eaten much of her skin on her face. She has recovered and is doing fine.

As we toured the beautiful facility (the absolute nicest we have seen anywhere in Kenya) we were given this sobering statistic: There are about 30 million people in Kenya. There are over 1.5 million orphans.

You do the math. They are the most sobering statistics I can think of; one of every thirty people in Kenya are orphans.

Your pal,

Steve

Your Pal, Steve

Dorm Mice
— *November 18, 2001*

When you have a dorm of seventh grade boys, you get many requests for pets. We've inherited a rather stupid dog for the term that enjoys moaning and sewer water, but she is never quite enough for 15 boys. So tonight, after a meeting, all our guys came home with mice they had found in the field. Nan hates mice with all her heart, so they thought by showing her the mice individually, they would win her over. By the fourth mouse, Nan was close to the ceiling. If you had heard their pleadings, you would have thought this was training for further lawyers. But we have held firm, and think we are presently mice free.

This week will be unusual; Thursday is just another workday. I'm sure it is the ugly American in me that is still shocked that Africans don't celebrate Thanksgiving, but it will be business as usual here. Since we are full up on our schedule, a kind friend has invited us over for a turkey dinner. Don't feel sorry for us though; did YOU get Moi Day off?

The cultural differences here are still striking to us. Nan has written about how taboo it is to ask someone if they are pregnant. Contrast that with the states, where everyone who is pregnant tells everybody they are. Our friend Grace told us that if we asked her if she was pregnant, she could hit us!

I experienced the other side of it this week. Some of you might remember Charles, the man who carved salad spoons and bowls for a demonstration for our dorm boys when we were here before. He has since died, and his son and an older friend came by yesterday to try to sell some of their wares.

After showing us what they had, the older friend informed me that Charles' son was 16 and was soon going to become a mature man. I thought about the states, and what that might mean. The only thing that came to mind was getting your drivers license.

But it was something quite different. The way you become a man in his tribe is to get circumcised when you are 17. And you have to do it without showing fear. And that was fine to talk openly about.

I'm afraid I would not make a good African. I showed fear just talking about it. And the flinch I had indicated that I would not be a brave member of his tribe.

I've always been kind of a rude guy, but even on my worst day, I can't quite imagine going up to some 16-year-old kid and asking `Yo — you been circumcised yet?'

Have a happy thanksgiving; if you are a guy, I trust I gave you one more thing to be thankful for.

Your pal,

Steve

The Road to Katie and Casey
— *December 3, 2001*

With all due respect, Nancy doesn't understand males. At the end of the term, we have our dorm clean up, and we write down the things they will need to do. On the list that she was going to actually GIVE to the boys, she had written: `Wash walls if necessary.'

Sadly, it came to me to inform her that I was 46 years old, and had NEVER felt like it was necessary to wash a wall. If the walls were bleeding, I would bet money that there wasn't a seventh grade boy on the planet who would take that as a cue to wash them. We removed the suggestion, made it a requirement, and finally passed inspection so they could go home for a month.

Before they went home, we had to have a contingency planning meeting. Because the US embassy was bombed in Kenya a few years ago, we need to have a plan in case of emergency. We all need to have one carry on bag with passports, clothing, and a few other items. I asked our dorm guys what they thought they should have in that bag:

- Hockey Stick
- Poster of favorite soccer player
- Candy

Not one of them thought that a change of underwear was a priority, which gives us reasons beyond the obvious to pray for peace on earth.

We've made a huge decision, and it was the toughest one we've ever made. In contrast, the decision to come to Kenya was a walk in the park.

I always always always wanted a daughter. I would not trade my sons for anything, but I wanted a daughter badly. My brother also had three sons, and threatened before the third was born that whatever it was, it was gonna wear a dress. His son Jon is a very handsome young man who would not look right in that kind of attire. He finally has had two beautiful granddaughters and has found his peace.

It had been on my heart for a long time to consider adopting. There are so many children who need homes in Kenya that it is hard not to consider it. But it was too soon after Stephen's death for Nan, and so it was something we put on the shelf.

When we returned to Kenya, Nan started to actively consider the possibility of adopting. As she considered the pros and cons, she came to realize that the cons were mostly fears, and she didn't want to be ruled by fear.

Then a friend of ours, a Dutch missionary who lives in Nairobi, stopped by and told us that he had adopted a child. Nan asked him: `Wasn't it hard when there are so many children to choose which one?' His response changed our lives. He said `It was so obvious.' When Nan told me that later, we both wept.

She then heard about twins that had been abandoned at the New Life Home, an orphanage for abandoned babies with HIV or Aids. When she heard about them, her heart leaped, and she knew they were for us.

As she told me, I wondered `Who IS this woman?' Nancy is a woman who would hit me every time I mentioned how neat it would be to have twins. Now she was talking about adopting twins.

We talked to JT and Matthew. One of them was very pro adoption, and one was very leery about it. We all went to the orphanage together, knowing it had to be a family decision.

There is so much need in this country. But you can't adopt children out of need. It has to be more than that, especially when you already have a family. I talked to almost everyone of my African American friends in the United States about the subject, and I know how controversial a white family adopting black children can be. I know how many issues we will face as a family. And I have had three children as infants; I'm very realistic how much work and sacrifice it will take to adopt four-month-old twins, especially at my age.

But as we walked out of that orphanage, our reticent child said `Let's get them both!' And beyond the needs and the desperation, one fact that I don't quite understand made itself clear to us:

They were supposed to be ours. They were our children.

We've begun the process of adopting Katherine (who will fulfill a long time dream of mine and be called Katie) and Casey. They were abandoned when they were three days old and initialed tested positive for HIV. HIV is transmitted by breast-feeding, and the fact that they were abandoned so early is probably what saved their lives. They now have no traces of HIV in them; a phenomenon that occurs in about half of all infants in Africa who test positive for HIV at birth. The other half develops full-blown Aids and die within a few months.

The process can take a long time, and so we would ask your prayers. We committed to go to northern Kenya for a ten-day trip starting Thursday, so we will be out of touch for a few days. Our hope is to have the children before Christmas, but whether that will occur or not is an open question right now. We will begin as foster parents, with the hope of adopting after a six-month period.

I wouldn't be honest if I didn't say there haven't been times of sheer panic and high anxiety regarding adopting these children. Half the time we have been thrilled, and half the time we have been terrified.

But in the end, it wasn't a hard decision at all.

It was so obvious.

Your pal,

Steve

PS Last time we were here, we got six, count 'em, six, Christmas cards. You can mail a card to Kenya for 80 cents. Family picture cards are especially nice; is this enough of a humiliating beg?

Squatting Through Northern Kenya
— *December 19, 2001*

We had an unusual opportunity. We would spend 11 days in northern Kenya, and go to some of the most remote areas on the planet. This wouldn't be a tourist trip, but a chance to see some different cultures that rarely get observed.

We rented a game tracker, a huge truck that can go over anything, and is accustomed to the non-roads of Kenya. In addition to that truck, eight other cars joined us. We camped the whole time, and had four days without access to showers. We went seven days before we saw a car that was not one of ours.

DAY ONE: We drove about seven hours to Mugie Ranch, which has lions, giraffes, and elephants. On the way, we stopped for a bathroom break; except there was no bathroom. I walked about a half mile away from the trucks, and felt very very self-conscious. I realized that I had not squatted since I was a junior in high school, and my squatter is not what it once was.

Day TWO: We went to Kurungu, about eight hours away. When we arrived, we were treated to a wonderful outside shower. You've never seen stars like you do in Kenya, and taking a shower after being on extremely dusty roads in an open air vehicle, looking up at the stars was an experience I will never forget.

DAY THREE: We went into the village in the morning. These are people who live in mud huts, and they share their huts with the infant animals they have. Most of the children wore little clothing, if anything, and many of the women wore no tops. Several thoughts came to mind:

- It was amazing how easily and rapidly you can get used to nudity. I went from being embarrassed to blasé, in under 15 minutes.
- Without being crude, national women without support who do hard work all their lives could end America's fixation on the glands in about 15 minutes.
- Poverty is a relative term. You would call these people poor by American standards, but they live in beautiful surroundings in a close, caring community.

We were invited to see the Samburu warriors dance, and it is quite the production. We were asked if we might be interested in dancing, and I thought `This is my big chance.' I actually got to dance with a large group of men for three dances, and I can assure you, my reputation for being the whitest person on the planet has not changed. From what I could tell, the dances consisted of jumping up and down and yelling.

It would seem hard to mess that up, but judging from the rather loud gales of laughter, I managed to do it. We videoed it, which I am sure will embarrass me all the rest of my days.

DAY FOUR: We went to the open-air church, and at the entrance to the church were dozens of walking sticks. These people are herdsmen, so they combine walking sticks with rungus, which is a hard wooden ball carved into the handle to be thrown at predicators. Worship is always interesting in another language, but the sincerity and wonderful singing carried the day.

After church, we drove to Korr, which is about four hours away. We were getting good at setting up our tents, and JT and Matthew did it rapidly. Unfortunately for them, they didn't close up their tents.

DAY FIVE: Matthew woke up with at least 60 mosquitos' bites on his face, with as many on each arm. We were taking malaria medicine, and although we don't think they were malaria-carrying bugs, we were glad we were being safe rather than sorry.

We went to see the Rendille tribe. They are known as being the Italians of Africa. They are very gregarious people, and I felt like I was running for office I shook so many hands. When I shook hands with the children, I would jump up and down, and it again amazed me that no matter what culture you are in, little kids like to giggle. These people live in the desert, and much of their liquid is cow blood. It was truly amazing to see how they could survive in such a brutal environment.

DAY SIX: As much as I can appreciate the beauty of different cultures, I am impressed of how important reading is, and the power of illiteracy to keep a people down. The missionary group here is doing an amazing job of teaching adults how to read, and reading can really transform lives. With many of the adults, they had no schooling at all, so it is a daunting task, but to see the determination of the people trying to learn would encourage anyone to soldier on.

If you've never read, how do you know what the front of the book is? The cover of their books shows the front of a person, and the back of the book shows the back of a person.

DAY SEVEN: We headed for Kalacha, which is on the edge of the Chalbi Desert. I saw my first mirage, and understood how easy it would be to be fooled. After driving for many hours, we arrived and one of the RVA students home with his parents showed me the Black Mamba snake he had found right near the campground where we were staying. He had it in a jar, and I was very grateful for glass in a way I had never been before.

DAY EIGHT: There is a pool of sorts at this campground, set up by very creative missionaries, and Matthew was so thrilled that he spent the whole day in the pool. I was the adult who watched the kids. Besides his grandparents, his friends and his dog, the only thing Matthew really misses is swimming, so he made the most of it.

DAY NINE: We headed back to Kurungu, and because it had rained, the roads were very tough to navigate. At one point, going up an unpaved 'road' our truck lurched so violently to the right that I thought we might tip over. We got everyone out of the truck, and after several minutes of being stuck, we finally got out. We were grateful; the African desert is not a good place to be stranded.

DAY TEN: We are in a campground where lions are unrestricted. Nan and I go for a walk, and a couple starts yelling to us to run because lions have entered the area where we are. We run, and find out later that it was waterbucks, not lions, but we do see several lions later.

DAY ELEVEN: When I started this trip, it was embarrassing to squat. I am now convinced I could drop trouser in the middle of Macy's the day after Thanksgiving and not think a thing of it. Is this progress or regression? There was a small latrine that one of our party left rapidly because of the black mamba that objected to the gifts offered.

Conclusion: How can you help without damaging what is precious in a culture? Some of the children we saw wear no clothing at night, and pneumonia is common. Part of the culture of one tribe is that the warriors can leave their spears in front of any hut, and then sleep with any woman within. Besides the obvious subjugation of woman, it is a way that AIDS is rushing through the area. Sanitary conditions are horrific. Children can often be hungry.

But so much of the cultures of different tribes are wonderful; close communities, close families, a love and understanding of nature that few of us will ever have. How can you keep the good in a culture but offer help to eliminate what is harmful? It isn't an easy question, and I'm not sure there is a formula, but I came away enjoying the different cultures and longing to help change what is harmful and deadly.

Much has been made of the cultural imperialism that so many missionaries once practiced, but what I saw where people who cherished cultures, and looked to see what was in a culture that they could learn from. It also made me see that pure Christianity, divorced from cultural influences, is the one thing that can truly change this country.

These are the heavy lifting missionaries. One couple works in a community of 20,000, and handled all the famine relief when the drought was on. They have to spend so much time just trying to survive and stay alive, and they have to do it themselves. I walked away in awe of their sacrifice, and of their love of the people.

Toilets look different to me now. I don't take them for granted anymore.

Your pal,

Steve

They Are Here!
— *December 23, 2001*

Saturday 23, December we went into Nairobi to the New Life Home and brought back Katie and Ben. Yes, I know we told you he was going to be called Casey, but he's a Ben! They home had named him Ben and all of us kept calling him Ben. We had no problem switching Betsy over to Katie, but Ben is Ben and so he shall be!

I was concerned that I might be ambivalent towards the babies. Actually I was AFRAID. But that proved to be no issue at all. Once they were in our arms and at home with us, they were ours in every sense of the word. No effort needed to call Ben "son" or to refer to myself as "mama"-it just is. But the first few days were scary, I guess is the word. We were tired (no they didn't sleep through the night at first, but happily they are now!), had some doubts, lots of fears, concerns about JT & Matthew, the full gamut of things. But JT and Matthew seem to be adjusting even more quickly than us! Matthew has claimed the role of chief bottle maker, JT likes to feed them and put them in the Johnny-jump-up.

Now that we are about a week into things we are really settling in together and enjoying these sweeties completely! I felt all thumbs when I changed the first diaper, but some 2-3 dozen later, I'm as accomplished as ever!

Katie is the firstborn and weighed more at birth. She has very delicate features and very little hair. In our humble opinions, she's beautiful! And she is sweet. Quick to smile and coo (although her happy coo is pretty loud!). She's also a bit on the feisty side, at least in comparison with her brother Ben.

Ben is a teddy bear! Even though he was outweighed at birth he has more than made up for it and is now a full pound heavier. He also has lots of hair, although he also has Steve's hairline. His smile warms up your heart and you've got to kiss him! He's a cuddler and Katie is more on the inquisitive side.

Their birthday is July 7 so they are almost to 6 months. Katie weighs a little over 12 pounds and Ben is about 13.5.

Our hearts are full, as is our family. God has indeed blessed us. Our Kijabe community has been so generous with us. We bought cribs and a great heavy-duty, double, jogger stroller but almost everything else from diaper pins to clothes and blankets and bottles has been given to us. Our Kenyan friends are also very pleased with the addition of Katie and Ben-they will never want for love or attention!

Your Pal, Steve

Thanks for praying with us and for us. We will send a photo very soon.

Our love and belated Christmas greetings to each of you,

Nancy

Always Follow a Schmuck
— *December 30, 2001*

My corporate philosophy in America was `Always follow a schmuck.' I figured if I followed a loser, I could be mediocre and still look good by comparison. I didn't do that in my last job, and it was embarrassing. My boss was a genius tech who by some amazing accident was also cool, and I was a dwarf by comparison.

The same thing has happened to me here. The director of finance is a force of nature, and he went back to the states for his daughter's wedding. Besides being an ace programmer and having twenty years of IT experience, he finds problems no one else notices and fixes them. Definitely not the guy you want to follow.

Fortunately, his second in command does everything, so I am supposed to be the figurehead for four months so people will appreciate him LOTS more when he returns. I didn't think I would do anything but attend a few meetings.

Then our bank got bought out.

We went to Nairobi to meet the new bank. We had called several times to make an appointment with our representative, and he was never available. They finally told us to just come in and he would see us.

When we pulled into the parking lot, guards with mirrors on large poles looked under our car to make sure we didn't have a bomb underneath. We went into the bank and were informed that our representative had been out of town for ten days, and wouldn't be back for another week. It's part of the Kenyan culture; it's best not to be direct. They directed us to a waiting room and told us someone would be by in a moment to help us.

After five minutes, I asked my friend how long he thought we would wait. He said five minutes. I told him `A coke says 45 minutes.'

45 minutes later, there was still no one to see us. I went into the lobby and said `We were one of the largest depositors in the other bank; might someone want to see us?' Moments later, we had lots of company. The new checkbook was still not ready, and everything that was promised to be grand fathered from the previous bank wasn't, so we have some work to do.

We still don't have a car here, and what happened to a friend of mine here illustrates the issues of buying a car. Cars are so expensive here, the `roads' are so hard on them, and so few Kenyans can afford them, that it is fairly common for people to buy 15 year old cars for fairly substantial amounts.

My friend bought a car from a dealer, and was in town when a police officer told her that the registration was incorrect and that he would need to impound the car. She called the dealer and he showed up with the papers, but they were the wrong ones.

The officer still wanted to impound the car, so she said to the officer `Tell the dealer to give me his keys to his car. The officer said `Give her your keys.'

She left with the dealer's car, and it took the dealer three weeks to resolve the issue. They finally got their car back yesterday, but it illustrates the creative mind it takes to play the game here.

We got the twins on December 23. Before that, we had to meet with a social worker. She is responsible for hundreds of adoptions, and she had missed several appointments with us. We finally realized that she didn't own a car, and she couldn't find transportation. We had guessed a lot of reasons for the missed meetings, but we didn't think that the head social worker for Kenyan wouldn't have a car.

We've found out that the twins were abandoned by their mother, and that the tradition of their tribe is to leave the children out for the wild animals to devour them. We thank God that their grandfather took them to the orphanage; when it is time to tell them the hard truth, we will be able to say that it was a family member that saved them.

The night before we got them was so full of anxiety; were we doing the right thing? Would it hurt JT and Matthew? Could we really do diapers and late nights at this age?

Once we got to the home and held them, all those fears went away. Until the first night and the first diaper. When you haven't been woken up by an infant in years, it is disorienting and jarring. The first few days were nerve racking. It took me several diapers to get back in the swing of things, and I violated the golden rule of diapers: assume every gun is loaded.

But after two days, they started to settle into a routine. We ended up keeping the name Ben instead of Casey; he is a big old bear of a kid, and Ben just suited him much better. There were 65 infants at their orphanage; once they figured out that they wouldn't have to wait in line to be fed, they seem to be settling down.

Several old friends wondered if my new son would be ignored because I had a daughter. Frankly, I had the same thoughts at first. But Ben is the sweetest guy in the world; he's someone you can't help but want to hold and be with. Katie is a little flower, and of course there is no prejudice when I say that she is the most beautiful girl in the world. She also makes a noise similar to Chewbacca, and that is when she is happy.

J.T. and Matthew are doing great with them, and the twins love their older brothers. Christmas was a sweet time. I don't think I could get away with giving a can of Dr. Pepper to J.T. as anything but a gag gift in the states, but it was a thrill for him here.

Nan's sister sent Matthew one of those electric balls that you can touch and little lightening bolts meet your finger. He has wanted one of those for years, and he as thrilled as he could be.

He was moving it the next day, and he dropped it and it broke. You always hate it for your kids when they break something they cherished, but it was hard on us also. You just can't hop in your car and buy a new one. It was just a hard lesson for him, and Kenya is full of hard lessons. We needed beds for the twins, and you just don't buy a bed. It's a process, and not always an easy or convenient one. They have to be made, and that usually means more time then you want.

All that being said, it would be hard to imagine a nicer holiday. The other night, Katie got up and started crying, and after I changed her diaper and fed her, I sat on the coach and let her fall asleep on me.

It just felt so right.

Steve

Letters from 2002

Battles, Wars, and Oiling Babies
— *January 6, 2002*

Life is all perspective, right? There is an old song that goes `One man's ceiling is another man's floor.' I have discovered the ultimate example of this.

Assuming that you are an adult who is reading this, I would also assume that if a large rat made its way into your bedroom, your response would probably not be `Sweet!' However, this was the reaction of my oldest son when he discovered the rat. The rest of the dorm quickly sprung into action, and `Rat Wars' began. They all got sticks, and invented many different traps to catch the rat. Nothing has worked yet, but I think this is the moral equivalent of a new video game in the states.

The battle is with six-month-old twins who act like they were abandoned at birth so bed is the ultimate enemy. The battle is getting them to sleep around the same time, and to sleep through the night. The best we have done so far is 5:30am, which I can live with because it is the time I get up anyway. Katie wakes up happy as soon as she is taken from the bed; Ben must be consoled for a period before he actually believes that he will be set free.

They are both good eaters; the first time I fed Ben, I thought after he drank the bottle, he would try to eat it. They have both settled down, and seem to understand they are no longer at an orphanage where there are 65 other babies and you get fed when they get to you, so it is no longer necessary to scream with such urgency. Don't get me wrong; they are still babies and they cry when they are hungry, but the urgency is gone. But almost everything sounds like a crying baby right now; I was brushing my teeth with the electric toothbrush, and Nancy thought it sounded like a crying baby.

The biggest surprise to me is how dry African babies' skin is. After you change diapers, you usually put some oil on their foreheads. After a bath, they get oiled down all over. I had lots of African American friends in the states, but I never remember this being discussed before. I guess that makes sense; if someone came up to me and said `Did you know our people suffer from dry skin' that would be an unusual topic of conversation, even by my standards.

Matthew and I climbed Mt Longenot on New Year's Day. I'm trying to do something special with each of the older boys so they don't feel left out because of the twins. (It is actually so busy in our house that they probably long to feel left out, but they are enjoying helping out right now). As we got to the top, I thought of the usual resolutions: lose weight, exercise more, read Proust, but as I prayed, I felt like this was the goal I was to have this year:

Don't make peace with the fact that there are hungry children.

We are behind on everything right now, including Christmas cards after I unashamedly begged for them recently. We will get them out; honest. But my heart for this year is a plan to go underground to provide lunches for schoolchildren. I will have more information about it soon, and hope you will consider it. But if 9/11 taught me anything, it was to put my cynicism away. I'm around hungry kids all the time, and I don't want to be jaded to it.

I honestly think there is a way to make an impact. I don't want to spend years of my life here and not try to effect a change.

If I don't try, I've made peace with the fact that there are hungry children.

Your pal,

Steve

Diaper Lotto
— *January 13, 2002*

Changing diapers with twins is tricky. You don't want to sit in nasty stuff, but you don't want to change them prematurely while an act of nature is on going. I call it Diaper Lotto, and at this point it is safe to say that I have not won any great prizes, but I have seen more works in progress in two weeks than I saw with all previous three children combined.

This has been a week to realize that the children growing up at this school have led different lives than I have:

- One kid's parents are stationed in Yemen, and he tells me that he met John Walker (the American suspected of working with the Taliban) when he was in Yemen studying multi-culturilism. John Walker tried to convert him.

- One of the girls in my English class informed me that her father had been offered 40 camels for her hand in marriage. (The father turned down the offer, feeling as if it was his daughter's decision to make, and eighth grade was a bit too young to get married).

- I asked a group of students how many of them had been evacuated because of war, and over half had. I asked how many had seen someone starving to death, and virtually every child raised their hand.

The twins had their first doctor appointment this week. We don't dress them identically, but for those fans of identical stuff, let me throw a bone to you:

They BOTH have ear infections in the SAME ear.

It is fun to see them changing. Ben got a haircut, and no longer looks like a detective from some seventies TV show. With his infection getting better, we are starting to see more of his personality. He likes to dismantle toys. Katie, except when she is put into the horror of bed, is happy and curious. She loves to go for walks and to look all around.

I should mention how much we appreciated all the cards we received; it was a real thrill for us. Thank you so much. We mentioned that Matthew broke his electric ball the second day he got it, and a friend sent another one. I really wish you could have seen his face; it was the best gift I received this holiday.

Your pal,

Steve

Your Pal, Steve

Merry...Whoops, Happy ... Now Wait...
― *January 29, 2002*

~~Merry Christmas~~

~~Happy New Year!~~

Happy Valentines!!!

There is something just darn special about being the VERY last to get their holiday letter done. We hate to mail until someone is leaving from this area because so much mail tends to get stolen, and we've had some life changes that are our excuse this year, but there were three major events for us this year:

1. The decision to return to Africa: leaving a great church, a wonderful job, beloved friends and family was so hard and so easy at the same time. We had a fantastic life in the states, but the bottom line was this: we are supposed to be in Africa. It has been confirmed to us in many ways that this is the place for us for a season.

2. September 11 changed everyone. For me, looking at pictures of firemen setting their faces as they charged off to probable death or injury made me want to throw off the cynicism and apathy that I've ingested for so long. The heroes made me want to be better.

3. Those of you on our email list already know, but we were led to adopt six-month-old twins who had been abandoned. Katie and Ben have been with us a month, and it has been a wonderful time. It has changed everything for us, but they have been good changes (with the possible exception of sleep deprivation). What we've noticed the most in the last month is that they know they are home, and that they know we are mom and dad and big brothers. It's just the most wonderful experience to adopt, and it has brought all of us closer together.

We can't look forward without thanking all of you for helping us do what we are doing. From kind emails to monthly support to toys for orphans, we have been overwhelmed at the kindness and goodness of our friends and families. Thank you from the bottom of our hearts.

It is going to be an exciting year. JT becomes a teenager next week, so we will experience what few will ever know: infants and teenagers at the same time. He and I are climbing Mount Kenya in February to commemorate this special time in his life.

We've gotten permission to begin a project that we hope will make a difference in this country, and we have lots of duties and responsibilities on the campus. It will be a year that will be full of about everything.

We're excited. Thanks for all you do. May it be a wonderful rest of the year for you.

We pray God's blessings on your new year too--

Seventh Grade Boys: A Study in Sensitivity
— January 27, 2002

What is it like to live with 16 seventh grade boys? Last week, about 14 guys were all huddled in one room laughing a laugh that made me nervous. As a general rule, all laughter from seventh grade boys is suspect; this was particularly nefarious.

> **Me:** What's so funny?
>
> **Them:** We all swallowed a bunch of Tic Tacs and now we're all tooting on Joey's pillow!!
>
> **Me:** Why are you doing it to Joey?
>
> **Them:** Because he's not here!!!

Since we've had the twins, about six of the guys go out of their way to play with them. About ten are indifferent. And there are several who I'm not sure have realized we HAVE twins.

One of the staff members had to leave because of an illness in his family. I asked my dorm guys to make a card for him. One of them wrote: `I hope your brother gets better but if he doesn't I hope you have lots of fun in the states.' And he was SINCERE.

But the other day, my oldest son was walking arm in arm with a Kenyan and a Korean seventh grader, and they were talking rather animatedly. I had a fleeting thought that they were enjoying the interchange of different culture, and in their own small ways, building a bridge that would enable all cultures to co-exist in joy and peace.

And then I heard them. They were trying to figure out how to build a whoopee cushion.

Seventh grade is its own culture.

Matthew had pioneer days at school. You really haven't experienced US pioneer days until you've heard Brits, Kenyans and Koreans trying to approximate what they think a rural American accent sounds like.

A church back home gave us shoes to give away to Kenyans. We had originally planned to give them to an orphanage, but there were so many adult sizes that we have been looking for people in this area to give them to.

We offered some to Grace, who works for us. Her husband is not working, and he has issues, so she is the sole provider of the house. There were about three dozen pair, and after she looked for a while, she excused herself.

The reason that she did is that she was overwhelmed with the choices and the opportunity. She simply couldn't believe that each of her children would be able to have a new pair of shoes, and that she would be able to choose from so many. Almost every Kenyan I know buys used shoes from the side to the road, and the choices are pretty slim. She told us later that her boys were so excited that they couldn't sleep that night.

I still take so much for granted.

Your pal,

Steve

Up Mount Kenya
— *February 13, 2002*

In Jewish culture, when you are 13, you are declared a man. In many African tribes, the rite of passage is to be circumcised. I don't remember my 13th birthday, but I wanted it to be something JT would always remember, and when he learned the African tradition, he was grateful he would not remember THAT for his 13th.

Mount Kenya is the second highest mountain in Africa. The peak we were aiming for was 16,500 feet. We left school on Friday and would be back on Monday. We left hoping to arrive by four o'clock, because we had a two-hour hike to our base camp, Old Moses.

There were 17 of us going. We hired a guide who would provide transportation, food, and porters. This being Kenya, we went about an hour when we had a blowout. It took almost two hours to repair it, so we arrived too late to get to the base camp, and stayed in a little house near the gate.

I should pause here and say my idea of a good vacation is a good book and a good beach. I'm not an adventurous type, and at 46, not in my best shape. I knew this would be a stretch.

We began the hike at 7am. Mount Kenya is untouched; there are no clear trails in many areas, and without experienced guides it would be easy to get lost. It was cool in the morning, so we had sweatshirts on, but by 9 we were down to our tee shirts. We walked for several hours, and it became increasingly clear that this was going to be tough. There were two other seventh grade boys, and they were far ahead of the adults on the trip.

Around noon we stopped at a glacier fed stream, where I drank the most delicious water I have ever drunk. By about this time, reality was beginning to sink in. We had at least five more hours of hiking to do, and it would get very cold once the sun went down. But it was extremely challenging hiking, and extremely exhausting. When we arrived at the bunkhouse, I was as tired as I ever had been. We were at about 14000 feet.

We ate some soup and some stew, and then went to bed. There was no electricity or fireplace in the bunkhouse, and since it was about 20 degrees, going to bed was the only way to be warm. We went to bed early because we were going to head for the summit early. The mattress was similar to the foam padding found on computer packaging.

We woke up at 3:00am. The plan was to get to the summit to see the sun rise. As a father of seven-month-old twins, I think that sunrises are VASTLY overrated, but we had a full day ahead of us, so we needed to get going. We left about 3:15am with the hope that we would reach the summit in about three and a half hours.

It was cold, and very dark, so we were climbing with flashlights. There were periods of time when the only way you could continue up was being on your hands and knees and crawling. The high altitude made you gasp for each breath. It was so much harder than the day before.

And people started dropping out. It was so hard, and so cold, and it was so hard to breathe, that eight people dropped off before the last hour. Experienced mountain climbers know the deception of mountains; just when you think you have reached the top, there is more to climb.

But both JT and I made it. When we got to the top, we embraced, and I cried from the incredible emotion of it all. JT started crying because he hurt so bad; he had an altitude headache, he was exhausted, he was hungry, and we had to climb down.

I've run several marathons before, but this was the first time I had thought through the fact that I was going to have to retrace my steps down this mountain. When you run a race, once you are done, you get in your car and drive home. It took another three hours to get down to camp, and at this point I was so tired that if a wild animal came to eat me, I would have shouted `Take me. I'm yours.'

The difference between a 13 year old boy and his 46 year old father was once we returned to camp JT ate breakfast and looked refreshed and was eager to go. I got back to camp and realized that I had five more hours of hard hiking, and I didn't know if I could do it.

We left the camp around 10:30, and returned to the base camp around 5. That meant almost 13 hours of hiking in one day. Around two o'clock, my feet stopped moving. I gave them a command, and they responded by saying something unkind about my mother. It was the most unusual I have ever felt; if my behind had caught on fire, I would not had been able to run to a bucket of water. And when a Kenyan carrying a huge bag ran past me with a cigarette in his mouth, it made me want to cry.

We finally got back to camp, and after a good nights rest, I felt pretty fine the next day. The two-hour walk to the gate felt good. This being Kenya, our van, which was supposed to arrive at 11:00 AM showed up at 4 PM. This meant the real adventure was to begin: driving in Kenya at night.

Driving in Kenya at night is dangerous because the bandits come out, but it is more dangerous because many Kenyans believe that headlights cause their batteries to drain, so many many cars do not use headlights. After several close calls, we finally made it home.

Final thoughts:

1. Why didn't I take more pictures? The only explanation I can think of is that I've been on business trips when I couldn't wait to get home to be with Nancy, and as soon as I got home, I would fall asleep. I was just too tired to do it.

2. Embracing my son on the summit, looking at his face with his realization that he made it and had pushed past his limitations was something I will never forget.

3. No one can take this experience away from me.

4. But I would gladly give it to anyone who asked.

Your pal,

Steve

Much More Blessing Than Sacrifice
— *March 4, 2002*

Adopting the twins has been such a blessing. It has also been a very revealing time for me.

So many people have said to us or written to us, "What a wonderful thing you are doing. Those babies are so blessed to have you as parents." But as is so often true of God, the total opposite is what is really true. What a wonderful thing God is doing for our family through these twins. We are so blessed to have them.

Yes, there has been sacrifice involved in taking them into our family. We are more tired, more tied down, and it's more expensive. But the blessings we are receiving through them, far exceed our sacrifice. Their smiles melt many cares and worries away. They, surprisingly enough, have drawn our family closer together in a special way. But the most important thing they are doing for me is helping me see more as the Father sees.

Unfortunately, one thing I see is how selfish I am as I bemoan the fact that our social schedule is empty these days. (Busy people just don't ask a family with twin infants over for dinner_) I'm not asked to go into town anymore. I don't get out of the house much these days and can feel invisible since I don't connect with people like I used to. Despite knowing this is a short season, I can get pretty whiny and self-absorbed, and God is showing me how very unlike His son, this is. Jesus was more than ignored--He was rejected. And He didn't have two precious, smiling babies at home to comfort him. Yet He continued to go about the Father's business.

I am also seeing others more as God sees them. I've mentioned how the missionary community has gladly and graciously given us clothes, diapers, toys, bottles, etc. But my Kenyan friends have helped me to understand a deeper level of generosity. There is a passage in 2 Samuel 23 where David, in the midst of battle wishes for a drink of water from the well of Bethlehem. His three mighty men went, at peril to their own lives, to the well and brought him back a drink of water. David does not drink it, but pours it out as an offering to the Lord. This passage puzzled me for a long time. Why on earth would he not drink it? They didn't get killed so wasn't it ungrateful to not drink it? Emily and Hannah and Florence and Miriam have opened my understanding of this passage.

Several of the women I buy vegetables from, will give me 2 bananas or 3 apples and say "Kwa watoto" (for the babies), and not accept payment. This gift just about nullifies any profit they made from my small purchases. And then today Grace brought to me a bag from a friend of hers. I've been with her friend Emily on 4 or 5 occasions. She is a sweet woman with a gracious spirit who lives without a husband in a one room home and cares for 3 young grandchildren whose mother will not care for them. In the bag was a litre of milk and 2 eggs. She gave it to Grace and told her it was for my babies. As I looked at that dirty bottle of milk and those 2 little eggs, I could only think of David saying, "Far be it from me, O Lord, that I should accept this_" I cried and knew I wasn't worthy of such a gift.

How can I ever thank Emily enough for her gift that so demonstrates the love of God? Perhaps by allowing the Father to work in me such selflessness and generosity, such trust in the Father to know that I can give out of want, and yet have everything I need.

Ben and Katie are doing well. They are growing and eating and even Katie is beginning to sleep well. They can just about sit up by themselves. Katie has cut 2 teeth and Ben is about to. Katie aggressively and purposefully rolls everywhere, and Ben rolls occasionally. And as stated earlier, they both have smiles that just melt you. Ben's smile makes you think you are the most special person in the world. Katie's smile is infectious and makes you think all is well with the world.

Yes, it is we who have been blessed in a very wonderful way by having Ben and Katie added to our family.

Blessings from our family to yours,

Nancy

PS The attached photo is of JT and Mt. Kenya (the mountain he and Steve climbed) in the background. Wanted to give you the big picture, not just the summit!

Irregular Verbs or How to Disgust and Educate
— *March 7, 2002*

Grammar is the most boring subject in the world to teach, and certainly to learn. But my daughter has given me great inspiration. She is the most beautiful girl in the universe, but before she does the deed she grunts in a manner that people miles away are aware of what she is doing.

So, when we are doing drills in class to identify irregular verbs, what do I make self-conscious eight grade students do? You've got it; they have to grunt before every irregular verb. It certainly has made the class memorable.

The babies are doing well. Both Ben and Katie's first words were `Da-Da' but it can mean `I'm hungry, I like to be carried, or an irregular verb is coming forth to the world.' They haven't connected it with me yet, but it is still a thrill. They both came to one of my English classes this week, and how they reacted was interesting.

Ben will go to anyone. Anyone is a potential food source or has something interesting that he can take apart. Katie is a little more particular, and several times cried for her Daddy to pick her up. Part of the fun of being at this school is that Nancy could bring them by easily, and that in the course of seven minutes, they were held by a Dutch kid, a Swiss kid, two Kenyans, four Canadians and two Americans.

This has been a week of learning how failure can bring success. Katie doesn't always sleep well during the night, and getting up with her along with the rest of the schedule has been exhausting. About every other year, I throw my back out, and last week, I couldn't get out of bed, so I went down to the hospital.

The Kijabe hospital is always an interesting place. The doctor was fine and thorough, but then it was time to prescribe medication. Since most of the hospital is run on donated medicine, he was handing me stuff and saying `This hasn't been expired THAT long' and `This will PROBABLY still work'; stuff you don't generally hear in the states.

It was great medicine; I slept 16 hours a day. My family loved it because I was incoherent when I was awake, and (according to them) told them three different times during the same meal how muscle relaxers could lead to constipation. But with twins and lots of other duties, it wasn't fair for me to continue on this schedule.

So after five days, I stopped using the medicine, and I realized how truly tired I was. I didn't go into adoption naively, but nothing can prepare you for how much time twins will take, and I was trying to do everything else without realizing that it wasn't possible.

And I was embarrassed to admit that I couldn't do it all, that by the end of every day I wanted to give up. The principal of the school, a kind man, ran into Nancy and asked her how she was doing, and she started weeping. Another administrator came over to the house later and said the school would like to offer us the day off on Friday.

And my response to that was `I've really screwed up, haven't I?' He kindly said no, this wasn't about screwing up; it was about sometimes you need a break, and we want to offer one to you. I was so embarrassed; it was like the big secret was out.

But once it was out, it was so freeing. I was reminded of how little I can do in my own strength, and that He delights to be strong in my weakness, and suddenly it felt like the weight of the world was off my shoulders. Nancy and I are going away for the whole day tomorrow, and it is wonderful to realize that we need it and can do it.

I don't like to admit that I am weak, but I am, and it is so liberating to be able to admit it. It's not like it's been a secret to anyone else, but I feel better than I have in a long long time.

It's like this whole year; nothing has been easy. Everything has been worth it.

Your pal,

Steve

Name The Cow And Win A Prize!
— *March 21, 2002*

Our date was great. It's remarkable how being away for a day can refresh your perspective. It was also the first time I had driven to Nairobi since we had returned to Kenya, and it's not like driving in Dallas. I dodged mule carts, sheep, matatus driven by escapees from the Asylum for the Criminal Insane, and pot holes that are so deep and so wide you can't do anything but bid farewell to certain parts of your car as you go through them.

We went to an open-air market to just walk around and see what they were selling, and I had a verifiable I am not making this up exchange:

Me: How much for that?

Vendor: One hundred thousand shillings. (For an item you could buy for fifty shillings)

Me: You must think I'm dumb and rich.

Vendor: I did not think you were rich.

We returned to campus refreshed and eager to see the children. Ben and Katie, after they eat, like to lie on a rug and play with toys for about 45 minutes. We lay them on their backs or sit them up, and put a group of toys between them. Neither is crawling yet, but Katie is a good roller. After she has reached every toy she can from sitting up, she begins to roll to the center of the pile of toys. She grabs one, and rolls back to her side to deposit the toy. Once she has retrieved every toy, she makes a move for whatever Ben has, and then suddenly all the toys are on her side. She doesn't PLAY with them, mind you; she just likes to have them all. Ben is surprisingly calm about all this, at least at this stage. JT and Matthew are wonderfully amused by it all.

What is the point of having power if you can't abuse it? I run the computer department for the first through sixth grade, and we just got done installing email capabilities for them in the computer lab. All I can say is: you've never been Spammed until a third grader get a hold of your email address. Consider:

- One kid who wrote `Hi! I don't know you' to everyone in the A's of the address book.

- Since we are using old Mac's, it is pretty easy to do VOCAL emails. One fourth grader got mad at a sixth grade girl and sang `London Bridge' TWENTY SEVEN TIMES.

Where this became valuable was when I realized it was March, and I still hadn't seen the Super Bowl. Someone had a copy, but he was being coy about letting me see it. Suddenly, after 100 kids emailed him regarding my unhappiness, I moved to the top of the list.

Remember, I have YOUR address also.

It is the end of term, and we always have a big dorm party. I made perhaps the stupidest announcement in the history of my life to my dorm:

`Friday night the dorm party will commence with a water balloon fight. At that point, you may not address me as `Uncle Steve.' I will be known as `Mister Toast' because I will be that dry at the end of the fight.'

The gory details are best left to the imagination. A grand time was had by all but one.

Several of our guys have already left for Madagascar, which is a scary situation right now. There have been lots of strikes and riots, and the airports were shut down for several days. Sending seventh grade boys back to that situation is sobering, but they were so excited to go back home.

We are in the third world. Some reminders are fun: we have had two-foot hornbill birds on our porch this week. And some are your worst nightmare. One of our staff members had been complaining of a kidney stone; the local doctors sent him to the hospital in Nairobi.

The Nairobi hospital gave him a clean bill of health. Since he was still in pain, he was sent back to the States. He is in critical condition and they have removed one of his kidneys. He is a wonderful man with a sweet wife and two beautiful daughters; his name is Jeff. Please remember him in your prayers.

He was given a clean bill of health a week ago in Africa.

Your pal,

Steve

P.S. A Kenyan friend asked me to help him purchase a cow. I agreed on the condition that I got to name him. He informed me that Kenyans do not name cows. I asked if it was part of his tradition to borrow money to buy a cow. He asked me `What do you want to name the cow?' And I thought, why should I get all the fun?

And so, we begin our contest. The best name for the cow will receive an original batik from a local artist, and the thrill of knowing that you have named the FIRST cow in Kijabe. Enter NOW!

Your Pal, Steve

Kow-Jabe!
— March 31, 2002

Several comments about the exciting contest:

1. Many of you have WAY too much time on your hands.
2. If someone is having a baby and I yell `Name it Steve or Stephanie' that is CHARMING. If you suggested the name Steve or Stephanie to name a COW, it is a sign of IMMATURITY and RUDENESS.
3. Those of you that decided to use this contest as an opportunity to insult me severely hurt your chances of winning.
4. We had more response to this email than when we announced that we were adopting Katie and Ben. It has made us ponder if we should have adopted cows, or had a contest for naming the babies.
5. There were over 150 entries, and it was not easy to come up with a winner. But in the end, with the help of our Kenyan friends, we picked the following:

Kow-Jabe

The winner will receive a beautiful batik, and I've enclosed an attachment of it as a sample of this artist's work. If you are interested, or just sore that you didn't win, there are more available. Just let us know.

We invited some special Kenyan friends to lunch, and after lunch, I told them `I have tried to understand your culture, but you must join me in understanding my culture. You cannot truly do that unless you watch `Star Wars' and eat popcorn.'

You haven't seen Star Wars until you have seen it with people outside your own culture. They did like Chewbacca the best, but we suspect it is because Katie sounds like Chewie when she is happy. They all seemed to enjoy the refreshments, but they all referred to it as `popcorns' which made Matthew giggle.

During the lunch, we asked all our Kenyan friends about Fred's wedding. Both JT and Matthew are going to be in the wedding (JT as a groomsmen and Matthew playing the wedding march) and Fred has assured us that it would only last an hour. I polled the rest of my Kenyan friends at the table and asked them for their guess on times:

Grace: Five hours.

Stephen: All day.
Cecilia: Five hours.
Joel: All day and some of the night.

The wedding is Saturday. If you don't hear from us, you will know why.

Matthew and I went down to the hospital to deliver some gifts to the children. We haven't been able to go as much during the term because of the twins, so it was special to be down there. We saw the usual sad cases, and I was reminded of what a friend of mine said about working in the African health care system: `This is the only place I've ever worked where malaria is a hopeful diagnosis, because at least it can be treated.'

While we were leaving, we heard a small girl, about 5, crying as she was being dismissed. I couldn't understand what she was saying, and I asked the nurse if she was still in pain.

The nurse said no, she wasn't in pain. The little girl was crying because the hospital was the first place she had eaten three meals a day, and she didn't want to go home and be hungry again.

Last week a Kenyan friend stopped by to see the babies, and was amazed at how big they are. She asked what we fed them. Nancy replied `Fruit, vegetables, cereal and formula.' Our friend responded `If you can give them all of that, then they will be very healthy.' Again, a reminder that a balanced diet is out of the reach of most Kenyans; once a baby is off of breast milk, it usually stops having a regular and balanced diet.

As we celebrated with a sunrise service this morning, I kept thinking about them. We are surrounded by people who do all they can to provide one meal a day for their family.

It's just not right.

Steve

PS Jeff was released from the hospital and is doing better. Thank you.

Energizer Wedding
— *April 7, 2002*

Fred begged us to bring the twins.

It will only be one hour, he told us again and again, and it won't be the same if the whole family isn't there.

And we were close to bringing them, until JT and Matthew went to the practice.

Matthew was playing the processional, and one tradition in a Kenyan wedding is for the bride to work down the aisle VERY slowly to show she is sad to leave her parents. After he played the processional SEVENTEEN times, she hadn't quite made it down the aisle.

That's when we decided to get baby sitters for the twins.

The wedding was to start at 10:00am. The boys went early because they were in the wedding, and Nancy and I showed up at 9:45am. The only people at the church were the groomsmen. No one else was there.

At about 10:45 the bride's car showed up, with about three dozen women surrounding the car, singing and dancing and having a big time. I think every bride should get a greeting like that. Another Kenyan tradition is that the bride is ALWAYS late for the wedding.

Around 11:00 am, the wedding began. The church was absolutely packed, and there were about fifteen white people there. The groomsmen came in, and JT looked very handsome in what looked like a Nehru jacket. Then the bridesmaids came in, with a very long, very choreographed walk that was pretty cool.

Some people think that a wedding rehearsal is unnecessary, but we saw proof of how the bugs can get worked out when Matthew started the processional. He only had to play it EIGHT complete times in order for the bride to get to the altar.

At this point, we looked over at JT and he looked even whiter, which was no mean trick. He had locked his knees, and he was close to fainting. Someone grabbed him and he sat down, but it was pretty close to getting interesting.

Then things got REALLY interesting. In a Kenyan wedding, apparently anyone with a camera can move to any location during the ceremony to take a picture, and at least a dozen people moved all over the place taking pictures. It got to the point when you wondered if they would rearrange where the bride and groom were standing to get a better angle.

There were five different groups scheduled to perform. Nine different groups did. When one would get done, another would begin singing from their seats and walk forward to perform. At this point, it was 1:00pm and it looked like it might never end. But after another 45 minutes, the wedding was over. There was a collection taken up to help clean the church.

After the wedding, they took about an hour of pictures from the church, and the whole wedding party then left to go to another location to take more pictures. So all the people at the wedding just lay down on the grass and waited. Nancy went home at this point, because it was close to dinner and the twins needed to be fed.

They came back around four, and the wedding lunch was served to all who were there, and it was obvious that for many, this was a major reason to attend. After an ample meal, the parents each gave three-minute speeches. This was three minutes in Kenyan time, so each speech lasted thirty minutes, and at that point, it just started getting more and more fun.

It was then time to give gifts. They played a tape that sounded suspiciously like roller skate music, and hundreds of people lined up to give their gifts. After the gifts were given, there were four different cakes cut, and I was one of the people asked to cut a cake. My cake was the friendship cake, and it is a big honor to be asked to cut a cake.

What I didn't know was that I was supposed to give a speech. At this point, I shouldn't have been surprised, because EVERYONE had given a speech, but I was not prepared, and I could tell by the laughter of my fellow missionaries that it was not was of my best efforts:

I am white You are not I come from Texas You live in Kenya But we are united in our friendship with our lord and with Fred and Sarah.

As I said `I am white and you are not' I saw two missionaries absolutely lose it, laughing so hard that I thought they might get ill. An hour later, I saw one of them and he immediately returned to the fetal position with tears pouring out of his eyes. At the time, I thought the speech was not as stupid as it sounded.

It didn't help my cause that as I cut the cake, I started yelling for fear of ruining the cake, which also didn't help my cause. As we were leaving later, every Kenyan I walked by started to scream like I did when I was cutting the cake.

At 5:30, it was still going strong, but my ride was leaving and I had to go. An amazing experience and a wonderful celebration; certainly not the time frame we expected, but a wonderful way to start a marriage.

One more thing. I've been a best man twice, and a groomsmen over a dozen times, but I've never had the honor I received in this wedding. At the bottom of the program (which is a story itself: how many wedding programs do you see with Cake Mistress and Convoy Mechanic?) there was a dedication to me. The last thing on the program was `To Steve, my first beloved computer teacher.'

Who says guys don't cry at weddings?

Steve

PS. We will be gone until the 15th. Catch up with you then!

Your Pal, Steve

A Chance for Change
— *April 21, 2002*

Here are the facts:

- The drop out rate in most Kenyan schools is about 65-70%.

- Most Kenyan children eat one meal a day.

- When a free lunch is provided, the drop out rate is reduced dramatically.

Here are some thoughts: - Most Kenyan children walk several miles to a classroom and sit all day on a bench without a back to it. - It would seem like one might be able to concentrate if you had some food in your stomach. - Without an education, there is little opportunity one can expect from Africa.

The World Food Program has established the following as the minimum nutritional requirements for a lunch program:

150 grams of maize (per student) 40 grams of beans (per student) A small amount of oil for cooking

It would cost me 1000 shillings or about $13.33 to purchase a 90-pound bag of maize. It would cost me 720 shillings or about $10.00 to purchase a 90-pound bag of beans. If I add cost for oil, a little salt and a few onions and my cost would be up to about $30.00.

For $30.00 dollars a day, I can feed 600 schoolchildren a nutritious lunch.

This is how it would work. The school would provide a parent who would cook the meal. The students would have to provide the bowl and utensils. We would provide the food and tell the school that we had given enough food to last for three months, and we would announce that to all the school and the parents, so any theft would have some accountability to it.

The problem with most aid programs is that most of the donated food doesn't get to the people it is intended to help. We could tell you stories that we don't need to get into, but the beauty of this is that all the monies go to buy local food and school children eat it.

There is no middleman. I will take the money, buy the grains, deliver the food and make sure that the students are getting fed. I don't get paid for this, and I don't want to be. All the monies go to feed the kids.

So, if you have been looking for something to help out, we think that this can accomplish the following:

- Decrease the drop out rate

- Increase learning

- The children will know it is kind Americans providing the food.

I will collect enough monies to commit to a school for one year. If we get more than we need, we will add another school. If you commit, you will own a school. If it takes 20 people to get a school fed, it will be those people's school. You can count on regular pictures and updates, and you can get an idea of what school is like for a Kenyan child.

I can't do this, obviously, without support. How many schools we cover depends on how much support we get. My hope is unrealistic, but I am so tired of seeing hungry children. I would love for this to get big enough that many many children benefit from it.

But we start with one, and if you are interested, please send a check made out to AIM and send it to AIM PO Box 178 Pearl River, NY 10965. In your note, please let them know that it goes towards the Peifer School Lunch Program. It is tax deductible, and they will send you a receipt.

The other need I have is a car. Several of the schools we want to begin with are in the valley, and there are no good roads. I will need a four-wheel drive van, and someday I will write an email about the adventure of trying to buy a car in this country. If you would like to help, you can send a check to the same place and include a note indicating it is for the Peifer vehicle fund.

I always add that I get a million of these requests a day, and if you can't or don't want to, it won't hurt our feelings. Do what you are suppose to do, and don't worry about the rest.

But I really honestly think this is a way for kids to get fed and go under the radar so it all goes to kids. I think it can really, really, make a difference.

Let's change the world, shall we?

Steve

White Sand and Black Bottoms
— April 25, 2002

This was new, taking a vacation with infants. We were all tired from the term and the excitement of adopting the twins, so staying for a week on the coast sounded wonderful.

Going to the coast involves an eight hour drive over some of the worst roads you can imagine, and for some reason, people who would normally gladly give us a ride were hesitant about driving with nine month old babies in the car.(One guy asked: `you taking BOTH of them?') We were going to rent a car, and discovered that it would be cheaper to fly with a special they had going on. Instead of an eight-hour drive, it was an hour flight.

There were two highlights of this trip. You don't have ANY idea of how much sand you have on you if your skin is white. Ben and Katie looked like they were sugar coated. They loved the sand and they loved the water; they just weren't wild about cleaning OFF the sand.

The older boys and I went snorkeling one day. We arranged for a local fisherman to take us to the coral reef. We went out in his wooden sailboat, which new cost him about 200 dollars. We had to walk a fair distance in the water to get to the boat (they carried Matthew) and on the way I stepped on a sea urchin, a spiky sea creature whose purpose is to make you bleed.

We got in the boat, and they didn't have snorkeling equipment, so we sailed for ten minutes, and they found friends that would lend us the masks. As we sailed into the middle of the Indian Ocean with no life jackets in a wooden boat, I thought `I am going to be arrested for being an unfit father.' But besides the bleeding and the thought that if the boat went down, we would all die, it was a pleasant trip.

We got to the coral reef, and it was shallow enough that the boys could stand in it. We say hundreds of tropical fish and all kinds of shells and starfish. It was spectacular; that was the only word for it. When we were leaving, one of the fishermen showed me the octopus he had caught in the reef. It came up to my waist, and I was very glad I was seeing it in the boat rather than in the reef.

The term has started, and our dorm boys give us grim reminders of what life can be like here. Two of the guys live in Madagascar and during the break at home, they were forced to stay in their houses because of all the riots going on there. One of them saw a machine gun fired on his street. One of the guys came back with malaria, and it's not the first time he has had it.

This is a beautiful place, but it can be so brutal.

Steve

Sacrificing Myself for Others: Nobility in Action
— *May 4, 2002*

For some reason I can't quite fathom, Nancy sometimes feels the need to spend time with other woman. The sixteen dorm boys are all remarkably sensitive and JT, Matthew and Ben reflect the compassion of the modern male. By now, you know how sensitive I am. And yet, Nancy will tell Katie almost everyday `Grow faster, little one. Momma needs another girl around here.'

Some of the ladies will have a birthday luncheon for each other, and it was scheduled to be at our house. Nancy made a wonderful pie for the dessert, and I had firm orders not to be near the house during the lunch, for strange reasons I do not understand.

As I pondered this, and the fact that I wouldn't get any of the pie, it suddenly occurred to me that maybe, just maybe, the pie hadn't turned out right, and how devastating it might be to Nancy if her friends rejected the pie, so I sent an email to all the ladies who were coming:

`Nancy's dessert did not come out. She would feel horrible if you didn't like it, so please say you are full when it's time for dessert. I will eat it when I come home, and praise her lavishly.'

For some odd reason, NO ONE believed me. Not one woman. Some made a point of telling me that they ate seconds, just on principle. And Nancy is giving Katie special vitamins to help her grow even faster.

It's hard to be sensitive.

Speaking of growing, Katie is beginning to crawl. She crawls as if she is being fired upon, with her being on her elbows instead of her hands, but she can get anywhere she wants to be, and many places she shouldn't be. Ben, although her twin, is almost three pounds heavier than her and content to do a bit of rolling and more thoroughly examine each toy he comes upon. Katie has two teeth in and one on the way; Ben has yet to have a tooth make an appearance.

Whenever we eat dinner, we have the twins with us although they have eaten earlier. Ben always looks longingly at our food, as if he is thinking `That could be mine.' If you saw him, you would not think he was underfed, but if you talked to him, I think you would walk away with that opinion.

Rugby has started, and JT is loving it. Most of our guys in the dorm are playing it, and as a dorm parent for 16 guys, I thoroughly approve of ANYTHING that exhausts 7th graders. Almost every kid comes home every night with something that hurts, and a big smile on their face. I can't wait until their first game.

There was a group of Australian schoolgirls that came to RVA this week. I volunteered to take them to the hospital and let them give some toys that some kind people have donated. As I tried to prepare them for what they might see, one of the little girl's eyes started to brim over.

And it was a rough week in there. Lots of hydrocephalus, and a burn victim whose face appeared to be almost totally gone; it was the only way I could describe it. Matthew went with me, and he always tends to go to the worst-case scenarios kids, but seeing her made him sick to his stomach and had to walk away.

One of the hardest things they have to deal with at the hospital is that whenever they treat one ailment, they find so many other things wrong. Because the water supply is foul and most Kenyans can't eat three meals a day, their systems tend to have amoebas and malnutrition is not uncommon, it's assumed. Because of that, their little systems tend to have more wear and tear on them than most kids would.

The one little Australian girl came up to me and asked `Why is it so hard for them? Why do I have so much and they so little? Why do little kids have to suffer?'

I told her I didn't know the answers, but that they were very good questions.

Your pal,

Steve

When You Have To Explain A Joke, It Must REALLY Stink
— May 9, 2002

My last email has been misinterpreted by so many people that I felt an obligation to offer an apology. It was entitled ` Sacrificing myself for others: Nobility in Action. I began the email with my attempt to swipe some pie from a luncheon that Nancy was giving for some ladies, where I emailed them and told them that it was no good so not to eat it; I would eat it later and in effect, sacrifice myself for them.

By the reaction we received, I'm afraid that I sound like a pompous jerk. While I must plead guilty to the jerk part, pompous people give me gas pains, so please know that while my attempt at humor failed, I was not trying to make it sound like I'm doing lots of wonderful things around here. I'm sorry for making that impression. The title of the email was supposed to reflect the pie incident.

I watched a Simpson's show once, and as Homer watches a TV show that fails to amuse him, he starts hitting the TV and yelling `Be more funny!'

My attempt is not to be funny in these letters, but to be honest and be real, and for how I have clouded the issue with the last email, I am truly sorry.

Your pal,

Steve

Your Pal, Steve

It's Hard To Be A Nazi In A Chihuahua T-Shirt
— *May 20, 2002*

Sometimes you just don't know what to say, and it's best not to say anything at all. Matthew was in a play in his class, and they were acting out a book they had read. When I asked him how his part went, he told me with great exasperation in his voice `It's really hard to be a Nazi wearing a Chihuahua t-shirt.'

We are in a pretty regular water crisis here. Part of that is from the deforestation of Kenya; only 2% of Kenya still is forested, and that has caused droughts and irregular rains. Part of it is we live around people who have to walk miles to get water, and most of the water they get is untreated and full of amoebas. Part of it is that RVA depends on a borehole well that is twenty years old for most of it water.

We collect our shower water and use it to flush, and fill the diaper pail. The dorm boys collect the shower water and use it to mop floors. We time our showers and try not to go more than three minutes. But there is always more that can be done, so we had a meeting with the guys to discuss how we could save more water.

They were very enthusiastic, and had lots of wise suggestions. The one that really got them going was when we announced that it took almost five gallons of water to flush the toilets. You could see the gleam in their eyes when they said `we'll go to the bathroom outside!!! You don't need ANY water for that!!!"

Again, sometimes you just don't know what to say, and it's best not to say anything at all.

One of our purposes here is to help Kenyans see the value of replanting. When you make a dollar a day, I'm sure your first thought is not to say: `Hey, why don't I buy some trees to plant?' But there is some dedicated staff that has begun to grow seedlings, and there was going to be a huge tree-planting day with the community on Saturday

This was a week to get discouraged, and find new hope in unexpected places. We planted four thousand trees in the community on Saturday, and many students in nearby schools came to help. They were required to come in their uniforms, so the boys showed up in suits. When I asked one kids if that was uncomfortable, he told me it was the only set of clothing he owned.

As we climbed the hills to plant the seedlings, we kept running into people who were cutting the forest down. Although it is illegal, it didn't seem to stop the hordes of folks who were destroying one of the last forests in Kenya. You had this little seedling in your hand, and you would see a huge tree being carried out, and the thought hit me `we are going to lose this battle.'

But then I saw Chuck Baker. Chuck is the shop teacher at RVA. He is in his sixties, and taught shop 40 years in the states. His wife died last year, and he decided to come out to be a volunteer. Just so you know about Chuck: he bought a house in southern California in 1969 that is probably worth a half a million dollars, and he has a nice pension. He could own a very nice home by the beach.

Instead, I saw him slip and fall twice as he maneuvered his way up the slippery slopes. I never heard him complain, and all he could do is talk about what a great day it was and what a privilege it was to be out there. And the thought hit me: `We're going to win; we've got Chuck Baker on our side.' I don't know if you ever had the thought that you weren't worthy to be around a person, but that is how I feel about Chuck.

Some friends back in the states sent $20 to us. They mailed it direct, never thinking that it would get stolen and try to clear their bank as a $2200.00 check. It was a reminder to remind you to never send checks directly to us, but it was discouraging.

Our older sons' school in the states sent plastic sheets for the orphanage. Orphans tend to wet their beds frequently, and the result is soiled sheets. You can't buy rubber sheets in Kenya, so it was a wonderful item for the school to have. But due to some miscommunication, they sent the items directly to the orphanage.

It meant that I would not be notified when it hit customs, and I could not receive the goods for the orphanage. The orphanage doesn't have a phone, so we had to rely on the mail to get notice of where we could pick up the goods. By the time we received the notice, between customs and storage, our costs were going to be $1500.00, which is more than I make in a month.

So it went that the pastor, his friend and I journeyed to Nairobi in his 1974 Chevy pick up truck that was shaking so badly that I didn't think we would get out of the parking lot. There were three of us in the front seat, and I sat in the middle. Because everything is a stick shift here, the driver had to reach between my legs to shift the car.

As we began the journey, with the car shaking and a man I had never met reaching between my legs at regular intervals to shift, we skidded and went close to going down a ravine. There were no seat belts in the car, and I realized I had the same thought I had had a month previously: I'm gonna die. But we had a wonderful time; it was my first venture in trying to tell an aggie joke to a Kenyan, and I guess some things are universal. I got real laughs.

After a two-hour trip to Nairobi, I announced to customs I couldn't pay what they were asking. I asked why bedding going to orphans would be charged customs. I've done lots of negotiations in the states and felt like I was fairly good at it, but I kept getting blank looks when I say `It's all for orphans in your country!! Why are you preventing this? Why aren't you encouraging this instead of fighting me on it?' They finally reduced it after a very very long discussion. Then we went to the storage company, who wanted almost $1000 dollars for storage.

We waited an hour, and then were told that no one could help us today, but if we came back on Monday, I could be helped, but the price would go up if we waited. After a long, long discussion, they said they would hold the price until Monday.

I spent the next week on the phone with the company. We talked over a dozen times, and after awhile, my great gifting in life won the day. They were so sick of talking to me that they agreed to reduce the price.

The pastor of the orphanage went back to town on Friday. Customs informed him that they had never agreed to a lower price, and that he could be fined for being late. We paid it all, but it was discouraging, and I felt like lots of missionaries start to feel: `why do I bother?'

But we finally had the stuff, so we went to the orphanage to distribute it on Sunday. Instead of just having a box of plastic/rubber sheets, they had a package for each kid. There was a blue floppy hat (so cool that all the seniors from RVA wanted one) a tennis ball (several kids asked me `why is there hair on this ball?') a sucker, a toothbrush and some washcloths. The kids were so thrilled: you could here them exhale as they saw each new treasure. And the best treasure was that there was a personal card in each package; I couldn't count the kids who said they had never had anyone write them a note before.

I was asked to say a few words by the pastor, and I got to say my favorite line: these were sent by people in America who love you.

Then I had to explain about the sheets. It was the first time in my life I've had a translator, and I'm sure he was grateful to have studied English as he translated:

These are your new sheets! If you pick them and make holes, I will come back and stand on your head. And then I will jump up and down!!! (As I demonstrated by jumping up and down, the 60-year-old pastor, who was translating, jumped up and down also)

It occurred to me that as discouraging as the customs charges were, the obvious work and care that went into those packages and the joy that the children had receiving them made me feel encouraged and grateful:

I'm on the winning side. I'm no Chuck Baker, and I didn't spend hours putting all these packages together and raising monies for the sheets, but I'd be proud to warm the bench for the people that did.

Steve

Me and Bill: Shakespeare in Africa
— May 28, 2002

The twins set our morning ritual. Lately, I've been lucky enough to slip away around 6 and exercise. I get back around 6:30, and I change them while Nancy prepares their breakfast. After we feed them, we get a blanket out and put them on the floor to play. Usually, we are all rushing about trying to get ready for the day, but on Saturdays, I like to play on the floor with them.

On a recent Saturday, I was playing with them when suddenly I realized that I had George Strait on the stereo. Babies are babies, and the truth is that when you have twins, you are too busy to notice their color. But suddenly I was very aware that my African babies were being subjected to country music. I thought `I can't help that I'm white, and I can't help it that I'm old, but I will not train my babies to love country music; that would be TOO weird.'

So I ran to the stereo and removed the country music (truth be known, I was the one that had put it in) and replaced it with Diana Ross and the Supremes. This led to another unfortunate problem. I have this odd compulsion to try to dance whenever I hear the Supremes, and the fact that I am unable to dance never stops me. I was in the middle of doing `Stop in the name of love' and noticed the looks on the twins; an interesting combination of morbid fascination and dread horror.

I pondered this until JT came to the rescue. `Don't worry Dad. Matthew and I don't like ANY of your music; why would the babies?'

I pondered whether this was depressing or reassuring, and decided it was both. And for me, coming out even means that I came out ahead.

We've been reading Midsummer's Night Dream in English class, and it has surprised me in ways I never expected. One of my best friends was Puck in our high school production, and I recall attending mostly to cheer him on, but I didn't read it until I was 19, and it was for a politics of Shakespeare class that could take the fun out of a kiss and a bowl of ice cream.

Rereading it was revelatory for me. It was funny! It could speak to eighth grade students where they lived! And it celebrated language it a way that could inspire budding writers to move beyond `whatever' as an explanation for character development.

If, like me, you haven't read it in awhile, what made it the most interesting is how it could speak to contemporary issues. One of the women in the play is named Helena, and she is so determined to be with a boy she tells him `I am your spaniel; beat me and I will fawn on you more.' I asked the question `Is this a good role model for a young woman? Is this how you would like your sister to act?' The resulting discussion was intense, and a look came over some of their eyes that I can't quite explain, but I guess I would call it the flicker of understanding.

At one point, as we were reading the play out loud, one of the characters said something stupid, and the whole class erupted in laughter. As they looked at each other in a kind of astonishment, I felt the very occasional joy that occurs when a student gets excited about something you are trying to teach.

It was short lived, as I discovered that the play they wrote for the eighth grade formal was how they all had to pretend that they liked the play to make Mr. Peifer feel good, but how they were bored to death by it.

However, I saw their eyes and heard their laughter. I know better. But Shakespeare impacted me more than them; they say you need to keep growing and learning, but it is easy for me to get in a rut and keep doing the same thing. Getting back to Shakespeare has been a great reminder; there are benefits in getting out of your comfort zone and trying to keep learning. Being challenged to think about eternal themes, beautiful language, and challenging characters has been a wonderful thing for me, regardless of how the kids responded.

I was in charge of Saturday detention. Those students assigned detentions have to get up at 8:00am and come to where you assign them. You can assign them to study, or do cleaning, or whatever you want.

I had two tough Kenyan kids, and I thought, `What would be the ultimate deterrent?' The solution was ingenious, if I don't say so myself.

They had to follow me around and pick up trash on the campus.

While they were singing Neil Diamond songs.

At the top of their lungs.

What didn't work is how into this the guys got. In my Surreal Moments in the Kenyan Hall of Fame, the top ten will surely include two Kenyan guys singing `Song Sung Blue' at full volume.

With this in mind, I will make many of you happy by letting you know that Nancy will be in the states this summer to help celebrate her father's 80th birthday. I will be here with the children.

And the Neil Diamond songs.

Your pal,

Steve

That Man Has A Bag Of Frozen Peas On His Shoulder
— *June 18, 2002*

We've got this genius guy here, someone who has managed to hook a microwave system to the only satellite serving Kenya telecom to improve our phone system. He is an accountant, programmer, engineer, etc.

He hurt his shoulder recently, and has had a rather painful recovery and therapy. I saw him walking the hall of the business office, and he had a bag of frozen peas on his shoulder. As you know by know, I am quite quick on the up take, and so I exclaimed ` That man has a bag of frozen peas on his shoulder.'

The explanation? Ice packs aren't easy to come by, and they are pretty expensive. The doctor told him that peas conform to your body shape, so just put some peas in a bag, freeze them, and voila!

It works, but it is still as strange of a sight as I've seen lately. It fits into Africa; making due with what you have, and being creative in the process. If you come to visit though, play it safe and skip the peas during a meal.

RVA is THE place to be when the world cup is going on. There are so many countries represented here that it's hard not to get swept into the spirit of the event. Nancy and I went to this tiny restaurant near campus. They cook over an open fire, chickens regularly walk through the door unto the cement floor, and there is no electricity.

But someone had an old black and white TV, and they rigged it up with a battery and rabbit ears, and there were twenty people watching world cup. It was my first sports bar experience in Kenya.

We had a short story in English class that dealt with young people becoming aware of their own mortality. I asked the class if they had any experiences with that feeling. One of my students from Uganda told me that there was a python in his village that had killed over two dozen people in under a month. He was riding his bike one day, and he thought he saw it and fled home. When they killed the python later that week, it was over 15 feet long. I was truly happy to be in Kenya and not Uganda.

They had early graduation for one of the seniors today. Regular graduation is not for a few weeks, but he received an appointment to the Coast Guard Academy and has to report for class soon. I've known Luke since he was a baby, and I will spare you the details of how much I cried.

But the thing that made me cry the most was every senior got dressed up to honor him. No one told them to do this; they just decided on their own.

This is such a neat place.

Your pal,

Steve

It Is Very Nice To Eat Sitting Down
— July 1, 2002

They asked the staff to provide prizes for the talent show. Most people made cookies, or something like that. Not me; I wanted something BIG; significant even.

Without beating a joke straight into the ground, what I offered seniors in high school was a CD of Neil Diamond's Greatest Hits.

This being RVA, the kids cheered mightily when it was announced, although several kids asked me if it was a first place prize or a LAST place prize. They had a special time in the show, and they asked who wanted the exciting prize. At least a dozen kids ran forward, but quickly sat down when they were told they had to SING a Neil Diamond song in order to win.

I just don't understand kids today.

Fred and I were talking, and I asked him where he got his haircut. He told me he was going to a different place. The reason was that the previous barber did not disinfect the blades, and he had gotten worms in his head. Something you wouldn't think about in the states, but a real issue here.

This is finals week, and so we celebrated by having three of the guys in the dorm and both babies come down with chicken pox. There is a shot you can give for chicken pox now, but you have to be one to get it, and the twins don't turn one until Sunday. They have been pretty miserable, and we are looking forward to them getting through it, hopefully before their birthday.

I was able to go down to the orphanage to celebrate a special event. One of our friends in the states raised money to replace the dining tables in the orphanage. A younger kid came up to me and said `Thank you. It is very nice to eat sitting down.' I didn't know what to say except what I usually say: it came from people in the United States who love you, but I couldn't quite get all the words out this time.

We are grateful for all the support for the school lunch program. We have enough to feed two schools for a year. Kamuyu School has 250 students; Nyankinyua has 350 students. They both have 1st through eighth grade students.

We worked with local church and community leaders, and they felt like these schools were the poorest in the area. Both involve exciting drives through non-existent roads.

I went to Kamuyu first. The biggest issue they have is that they have no water. They are trying to build a tank which would collect water in the gutters of their buildings during the rainy season, but they do not have the funding to complete it. They cannot offer a drink of water to a child. Many of the children walk several miles to go to school, and they do it without any water except what they can bring themselves.

Next I went to Nyankinyua. Both schools are similar in structure. They have rock walls, no windows and dirt floors. At Nyankinyua, they were growing seeds in the floor of one classroom. I've enclosed a few pictures of what the classrooms look like.

When I told the headmaster our plan, he began to weep. He told me that it was so hard for him to see children be so hungry, and he was very grateful to have the help. We will begin in September, because the term is almost over.

As I drove away, I passed some children who were still walking home, and they had already walked four miles. None of the children had shoes.

This is what I signed up for. I am so grateful for all your help. I'll be going to the schools each month to get updates, and learn what a day is like for the children.

The adventure begins September 2nd.

Your pal,

Steve

Broken Cheerios Need Not Apply: The Twins Turn One
— *July 7, 2002*

Ben and Katie turned one on Sunday. It was a festive day, with them eating their first piece of cake (Katie put her finger in the frosting and licked them; Ben ate his cake and then started looking at Katie's with heightened interest.)

Katie is pulling up but not quite walking; Ben is crawling but not as ambitiously curious as Katie is. He is content to thoroughly examine one toy for a long time; she needs to see everything.

Perhaps the biggest difference is how they view Cheerios. If you can find them here, they are very expensive, but they are a good food for little fingers, and a friend gave us some. Katie then displayed a new facet of her personality:

She will not eat broken Cheerios. Somehow, I don't think that it would be out of line in saying that broken Cheerios OFFEND her. Ben, on the other hand, thinks of her pickiness as manna from heaven. We have not seen the bottom limit of how much Ben might be able to eat. They complement each other.

The funnest part of the twins may be the older boys, who continue to enjoy them and add a unique fabric to the relationship. Whenever JT calls Katie `hey pretty girl' I get choked up. Matthew loves them and is getting quite good at putting Ben down for naps. I've said it before, but it has just seemed so natural. (When I get woken up at 2am, that is the small exception to that rule)

When we were in Africa before, we came for a year and left. I knew we were returning to the same house, the same church and all our family and friends. This year is different.

There was a staff tea today for the staff that are leaving. There are over forty people leaving; almost 40% of the staff. Some are just going for a year, some are leaving the missionary field for good, and some are retiring.

This is a small community; that has lots of good and some bad. A single neighbor has almost every move under scrutiny as he attempts to date another single here. If I had a problem with a kid in a class, the whole community knew about it.

But the small problems are dwarfed by the wonder of most of the folks here. It may just be that we are united by the difficulties of life in Africa, or our common purpose puts petty concerns where they belong, but I really feel a great deal of love for most of the staff here, and it was hard to say goodbye.

One of them in particular has inspired me this year. She was at RVA when she was a little girl for one year while her doctor father was a volunteer at the hospital. She had always wanted to come back, and made plans to come back in August of 2001. Her plans were somewhat altered when her boyfriend proposed to her just a few days before she was planning to come out.

And she came out anyway. I just can't quite imagine being engaged and leaving for a year, but she did it. Her fiancé,e ended coming here for the second and third term, and I thought about the sacrifice and hard work they did being here rather being home and planning their October wedding.

This is a tiring place, and they leave in a week with lots and lots to do and fatigue instead of energy planning their big event. I hope they don't, but I can imagine they sometimes wonder if they did the right thing.

When you see someone sacrifice for the cause, it just makes you want to be better. I just hope they know that their sacrifice has made me want to be better. But it's hard to see people like that leave.

Goodbyes hurt.

Steve

PS. The New York Times puts their corrections on page 27. Not me!! Here are my latest errors:

1. I wrote about the phenomena of someone putting frozen peas on their shoulder. It turns out that my mother in law has done that, one of my best friends in high school has done that, and basically everyone I have ever known wrote about frozen peas. I don't know HOW I missed it.

2. There are pythons in Kenya. There was a 12-foot python killed a mile from one of the schools we are going to be working with I wrote recently about a student who had a python killing people in Uganda, and I remarked how I was glad I was in Kenya and not Uganda. Now I'm not sure what I would write.

3. This is the big one. I managed to tell the time and address of Nancy's potluck in Dallas, without telling the date. Sometimes you wonder if anyone reads your emails, but this was proof that people read it, because almost everyone managed to call me a

big dope, in a very nice way. Anyway, Nancy will be in Dallas August 2nd-4th. The potluck in on Saturday August 3 at 1 at Colleyville Christian Fellowship at 3508 Glade Road in Colleyville, TX. (817-354-5757) Anyone who hates potlucks can come at 2 pm.

You Are My Favorite Student
— July 16, 2002

For the last day of school, I borrowed something from Erma Bombeck, and modified it for my classes. I started alphabetically, and told Ha-Sun Ahn: `You are my favorite student. I appreciate your brilliance in grammar, your witty writing, and your hilarious speeches. Please don't tell anyone in the class that you were my favorite student.' I moved on to Ryan and said `Ryan, you were my favorite student. I loved your accents when we read out loud, I appreciated how hard you worked, and your insights on Shakespeare were unique. Don't tell the others.'

By the third kid, I was pretty misty, and so were they. It was a remarkable year, and I'm very grateful that I had the opportunity to teach. As glad as I am, I'm gladder that a real teacher will be teaching the eighth grade next year. I'm moving on to other opportunities within the school.

One of our first opportunities was to get Jessie, the dog we had before, back with us. The reality of the coming and going of this place is that there are lots of dogs that are looking for a home. Jessie's owners are returning to the states for good, so we have Jessie, the co-dependent dog, back with us. Last night JT and Matthew slept over at friends' homes, and Jessie moaned so much that we had to let her sleep in our room. She can't stand to be without people around.

A friend here adopted a child a few weeks after we did, and the harrowing process they have gone through to return home has been sobering and frightening to us. Unlike us, they are returning to the states this month, so they have had to accelerate the process, and I can only liken it to a go-kart that you try to make go 100 miles an hour; some things just weren't meant to go fast.

In Kenya, you are supposed to foster care a child six months before you can begin the adoption process. Since they were leaving in July, they asked if it was possible to speed it up. They were told it was possible, so they began the process of adopting Reed.

In April, the laws affecting adoption changed in Kenya. The problem was that the courts did not know how to interpret the new laws, so they halted all adoptions. This meant that in the whole country of Kenya, no adoptions were granted for two months.

Keep in mind that the latest estimates of orphans in Kenya are now 1.4 MILLION children, and shutting down the courts for several months starts to take on huge dimensions. What it meant for my friends were dozens of trips to the US embassy, to the Kenyan court, to the lawyers to try to get the adoption formalized.

With a week to go, they were faced with the real possibility of leaving their son behind until they could get a court to schedule a hearing. Doing an international move is one of the most stressful things you can do; trying to do it while you battle the bureaucracy is the toughest thing I can think of. Someone in the court suggested that they leave their baby with someone and come back later to get him. Can you imagine leaving your baby behind? They are both professors at Spring Arbor College and were on leave for a year; they have to go back, but of course they couldn't leave their son behind.

This week, they petitioned the court for an emergency ruling, and a miracle occurred. The court granted them full legal custody. But their tickets were for Thursday, and between now and then, they must get a passport, a visa and several other sets of paperwork before they will be allowed to leave.

Roger got malaria in December, and stress now tends to make him weak, so I volunteered to go with him today. First we got a tire fixed that went flat yesterday when he was in town. Next, we went to the attorney's office to get the formal notice of adoption from the court. After waiting an hour, he received the paperwork.

Next we went to the US embassy to begin the process of applying for a passport for Reed. Next we went to immigration services to apply for a visa. We waited several hours, and the lawyer's aide who was supposed to be there never showed up. We went back to the lawyers' office who told us that the aide had not been able to get a ride so he walked to the immigration office. We drove back and couldn't find him.

Tomorrow Roger still has to try to get everything done, or they will forfeit their tickets. This is not a wealthy couple; working at a small college does not make you rich. The cost to change their tickets will run into the thousands of dollars.

I know that any African country has to be sensitive to white people taking children out of its borders. What happened in the past is horrific.

But there are so many children that need families, and need them fast. The process will discourage so many from trying. It is a tragedy, and a stupid, needless one.

Roger's perspective was helpful. All he could talk about is what happened the night before graduation. One of the seniors' fathers took ill during a party for seniors and their parents. He died later that night. Leaving RVA is tough for boarding school kids; to leave and have your father die is so devastating. He kept referring to her, and I really appreciated that he would think of someone else at a time like this.

We begin the adoption process this month. We are not scheduled to leave the country for two more years, so we don't have a time frame that is as difficult as Roger has. But because we have twins, no one can tell us a cost. I asked two different lawyers today the cost to adopt two children, and neither could tell me; they don't know if they will be treated together or as two separate adoptions according to the new laws. We don't know the costs, or the time frames, or the process. It's kind of scary. The only good thing is that no one else knows either, so we have a lot of company.

Nancy leaves on Sunday for the states for three weeks. There are many emotions connected with her leaving. I've never been away from my bride longer than a week in 17 years, and it's difficult to imagine being away from her for that long. On the other side, we are thrilled that she can see her dad and lots of family and friends.

The older boys have had one of their most unique arguments ever in anticipation of her leaving:

JT: No, I don't WANT her to eat THERE.

Matthew: But it's my FAVORITE.

Me: What's going on?

JT: Matthew wants Mom to eat at Fridays for lunch, and I think she should eat at Arby's instead.

Me: So you guys are fighting about where Mom will EAT when she is in the states? JT and Matthew: Vigorous nodding.

In essence, the boys are hoping to EAT vicariously through their mother while she is in the states. I'm not sure how that works, but I can assure you, the discussion was passionate. Both boys have made lists of items that they want her to bring back to Africa. JT's list is so large that I'm afraid of her getting a hernia trying to lift it all.

And, of course, I must be honest. One-year-old twins can keep BOTH of us really really busy. When I think of everything that needs to be done, a deep sense of fear begins to rise within me.

Then I remind myself: I change most of the diapers; I give all the baths; I'm a modern Dad who CAN do it.

Then I think of earlier this week when I was on the floor with the babies when Ben hit Katie on the head with a toy which made her cry and so I picked her up but then Ben threw up and immediately began to crawl towards it to examine it so I picked them BOTH up and went into the other room and got a phone call and forgot about the mess and both managed to thoroughly examine all of it.

So, as a modern man, I do not face the next three weeks without my wife with fear.

But with panic.

Your pal,

Steve

PS. Nancy will be in Dallas August 2nd-4th. The potluck in on Saturday August 3 at 1 at Colleyville Christian Fellowship at 3508 Glade Road in Colleyville, TX. (817-354-5757) Anyone who hates potlucks can come at 2 pm.

I've Got To Go Tie The Goat
— *July 28, 2002*

Until Kenya, the best one I ever heard was a professor at the Naval Academy. He excused himself from a meeting because `his ship needed to leave the harbor'. I was puzzled until I saw him leaving the restroom.

The older boys and I are taking Swahili lessons while Nancy is gone, and he confirmed to us something that she had told us earlier. In Kenya, if you've got to go do your duty, you excuse yourself by saying `I've got to go tie the goat.'

Of course it has caught on with the boys. You would think we had a zoo by the way they talk, but I think it will be part of our family tradition. I've heard so many variations of goat phrases from them I can't hardly believe it. A goat roast has taken on a new meaning.

TWINS 2, MODERN DAD 0

It's now been a week since Nancy has left, and like most things in life, the anticipation was worst than the reality. The babies have slept the night every night this week, and problems have been few. JT and Matthew have been wonderful helpers, and they have made it fun for me and the babies. We really miss Nancy, but I will always treasure this special time I've had with my babies.

As a modern dad, I have learned three things this week:

Principle One: As long as it doesn't hurt, anything baby's wear is ok. I managed to put Ben in an outfit that was completely backwards; it was like a sweatshirt with the place for your hands at waist level. Except that it was backwards; I had managed to put it on the wrong way and he wore it all day that way.

I discovered my error at noon, and I examined him to make sure that it wasn't causing any discomfort. When it wasn't, what's the point of changing? Colors are another story; my wife still dresses me, and I struggle with color combinations. I have told Grace that `oh, that is cool in the United States now' so many times that she doesn't believe me, for some reason. But neither baby is hurt, and that is all that matters.

Principle Two: If you have to bet between brute force vs. lightening speed, it's a tough call. Katie is almost walking, and can move like the Flash when she wants to. Ben is crawling, but he is pretty slow compared to her. Katie will crawl OVER Ben if he is slowing her down.

But she is not as successful in swiping toys from Ben anymore. Ben probably weighs three pounds more than Katie, and if he has his hand on a toy, she can't get it away anymore. He has a death grip. What is happening more and more is that he gets interested in something she has, and will grab it away. When she used to do that to him, he would just sit there and look at where the toy was. Now that he swipes it from her, he does the same thing: he sits and plays with the toy, while she rages. He pays no attention to her, but not in a rude way. He is just focused on the new toy.

Principle Three: Jealous dog = three children

I'm on the floor playing with babies. After awhile, they crawl away. Katie comes back and wants to sit on my lap. I pick her up, she cuddles for a few minutes, and wants down. Ben ambles on by, wants up, says DA DA DA several times, and then wants down.

Then the dog jumps in my lap. This has happened FOUR times this week. The babies have a little truck book that you can squeeze and it will beep. If I beep the book, all THREE of them come over to beep the book, Jessie with her nose.

I had a semi-funny story to end this with, but it has turned out not to be funny at all. A friend here went to get her license to drive a bus here. After paying so much money to the trucking company, she spent virtually no time behind the wheel of a bus. The bus at the school was decrepit and she didn't even get out of first gear. She went to the police to take her test, and instead of testing her, they asked her how long she had been driving. When she said `20 years' they said `That is good' and issued her the license. She never got behind the wheel of a truck. The trucking company just paid off the police.

It was funny when she told me the story, but this week, two people I know have been killed on the roads in Kenya. When you drive here, you often wonder how people ever got their licenses. I think I know now, and it's another little thing that is so brutal about this place. It sobers me up about small sins in my own life; they can grow to become such horrible things. The guy who passes people without testing their skills doesn't think of it as a big thing, but I know two widows that shouldn't be.

Your pal,

Steve

PS. Nancy will be in Dallas August 2nd-4th. The potluck in on Saturday August 3 at 1 at Colleyville Christian Fellowship. Anyone who hates potlucks can come at 2 pm.

Tea Party Girl
— *August 28, 2002*

The thing that is causing the most tension in our household is not that school has started, not that we have 16 8th grade boys living with us, but Katie. My older boys are outraged with her.

She can say Da-Da and Mama. But her third word was not JT or Matthew.

It was Jessie.

The dog.

This has NOT gone down well with the boys.

Katie has also caused some tensions with Nancy. Although I was the one who really pressed for a girl, Nancy has discovered within herself an intense desire to have tea parties with her female child.

But what we have discovered about Katie is that she is a bread fanatic. After the babies have eaten breakfast, they play on the floor for a half hour and then the rest of the family eats breakfast. We put them in their chairs and give them cheerios.

Until Katie sees the toast. Then she makes a series of long deep guttural noises indicating that she wants more bread. I can't think of a way to suggest what the sound is like, except you might hear it in someone who lacks fiber in his or her diet. Every time Katie makes the sound, JT says `There is your tea party girl, Mom!'

I'm working in Guidance this year (and at this point, may I suggest that all of you who have hilarious things to say about that remember that taking too easy of a shot is not a CHALLENGE) and with school starting, it has been busy. Since I come from corporate America, I had not realized how many classes get changed because Ha-Sun is in period one biology and I can't stand how she flicks her hair back after she finishes a test so I need it fourth period. It's been eye opening.

We are set to deliver the food on Saturday. Coordinating food delivery, purchases, and strong arms and backs (each bag weighs almost 200 pounds) has been a great challenge, especially when dealing with people who don't have phones and emails. This has been a typical conversation.

ME: Do you have beans?

THEM: Yes, many bags.

ME: I agree to your price. NEXT DAY

THEM: I do not have any beans.

ME: Why did you agree to sell them if you do not have any?

THEM: I thought I might.

That has happened to me several times, and it stems from people hoping they can find beans and sell them to me even if they don't have them. Because my car can't handle the three tons of food we are buying, I have had to hire a truck and driver, and the negotiations have been fascinating:

ME: I will pay 11,000 shillings.

THEM: And my lunch.

ME: OK

THEM: And my dinner.

ME: No

THEM: I will cancel.

ME: Good.

THEM: I do not want lunch either.

When I was in Kenya before, the life changer was delivering food to a school and seeing all the children lying on the ground. When I asked the teacher why, she told me that it was Thursday, and most of the children hadn't eaten since Monday, and when they sat up straight, they fainted.

We're not in a famine now. This is a long-term investment in children staying in school, but I can still see those children lying on the ground.

Your pal,

Steve

We're Not Even In The Race
— *September 3, 2002*

I guess I say this a lot in these emails, but I've never had a day like Saturday in my life. The drop out rate in Kenya is almost 70%, but when lunch is provided, the numbers tend to drop dramatically. We hoped to decrease the drop out rate and help children learn a little easier.

The plan was that all the maize and beans would be delivered to the orphanage where they had a guarded locked room. On Saturday morning at 8, I would bring some strong young backs and we would load them in a truck we rented, and deliver it to two schools.

By 9 the truck was there, and the 23 bags of beans had been delivered. But the pastor, who knew how to get to the schools, was nowhere to be found and the maize had not arrived. I really didn't know what to do, and so I went in the car and tried to find a woman that had bid on the maize. While I was looking, the pastor called me on the cell phone and told me he was ready to go.

I headed back, and the maize showed up in a large truck. (75 bags of maize, each bag weighing about 200 pounds, take up LOTS of space) I had paid the guy half the money, but he had not delivered it on Friday when he promised, and I didn't have the money with me.

Me: I will pay you on Monday.

Him: Pay me now, or I leave.

Me: Then leave half the maize; I've already paid for that.

Him: Just go get the money.

At this point, I knew it would take me an hour to go get the money. Fred was with me, so I told the guy `I will give Fred a note and you can go with him to my house and my wife will pay you.' He agreed, so we transferred the maize and finally left to go deliver the food.

Except we were on Kenyan time. After a good ninety seconds of driving, the pastor told me to pull over, because he needed to buy some food for a conference, so we waited twenty minutes while he purchased food.

It was easy to catch up with the truck. They had been pulled over by the police because it was in poor condition. I got out of the car and explained the situation to the police, and they said we could go.

I have never driven a four-wheel drive vehicle before. Basically, I was a pretty boring guy before I came to Africa. But we pulled off the main road, and quite soon I realized that I was driving like I had never driven before. I went through two streams, was backed up by a donkey cart, and saw several zebra and gazelle running near the school.

The first school we went to was Nyakinyua. It is a school of about 350 children in a poor, poor area. Right behind the school, ten miles away or so, is the telecom dish that serves all of Kenya. How odd must it be to be so poor, and see such great wealth so close to you. We were able to deliver all the food. The headmaster was so grateful, and large numbers of children kept coming up to me and asking: `Is it food for us to eat?' When I would tell them yes, they would jump up and down.

At this point, I started to know the difference between a 20-year-old Kenyan and a 47-year-old white guy. It took me and two other smaller guys to lift one bag. Everyone else was putting it on their backs. It would have broken mine in two.

The pastor told me there was a third school he wanted to add, and since we were near the school, he asked me to drive by it. But once we were within a mile of the school, there was no road or anything close to a road to get to it. The school was all wood, with dirt floors, and no windows. It was the poorest school I've seen. It is called Namuncha School, and it is attended primarily by Masai children, who live in mud and dung huts. They only have about 150 students, so we had enough to provide them food too.

The other schools are made of brick. Namuncha was made of wood, with no windows and dirt floors. It was almost impossible to believe that children would spend large parts of their days in a place like that.

We then passed by the pastor's church, and unloaded the food he had purchased. I was invited to eat lunch with them, which consisted of cabbage, beans and cooked carrots. It was good food and fun conversation, although three different times I would yell `It's time for an English break!' and they would have to speak in English for five minutes.

After our lunch, we started towards the third school. Have you ever been in fog so thick you couldn't see in front of you? That was how I was but it wasn't fog.

It was dust.

After a few minutes, the pastor said to me in his quiet voice: `If you go further, we will not live.' And darn if there wasn't about a 30-foot drop off right in front of me. I slowed down.

We got to the last school, Kamuyu, and delivered the food. What struck me more than anything is where the children go to the bathroom. I hope the picture captures the sanitary conditions for 250 children with no water.

We started back home, and I noticed that I was sore in the same way you might be after riding a horse for the first time. I was sore in ways I had never been before. It was almost like I had a blister where the moon don't shine, and I'm sure it was from going up and down all day long on the rough roads. There are bad aches and good aches; this was a good one.

About 800 children, most of whom don't eat breakfast or lunch, will have a hot, nutritious lunch for the next three months, thanks to all of you. I'm so grateful for what you did.

There is a big conference in South Africa next week, and one of the issues is development in the third world. Colin Powell, a man I respect as much as I respect anyone in the world, was quoted as saying that `We are in a marathon, not a sprint.'

I understand what he means. But when I read the quote, all I could think of was, if they were his children or my children, we would run like we were on fire.

When children have to live like this, and we know about it and let it continue, we're not even in the race.

Your pal,

Steve

Africa Is Whiter Than Indiana
— *September 8, 2002*

Several years ago, I signed a contract with a company in Indiana. To celebrate, they said they wanted to go a Mexican restaurant. I had lived in Texas for years, and told them I ate lots of real Mexican food, and we could go someone else. They insisted, so we went.

When the waiter came over, he asked if I wanted to hear the specials. I said sure, and he said `We've got (I'm going to write this like he said it) fa-ja-tas. At that point, I knew what I was in for. I would say it was the whitest meal I had ever eaten.

Until yesterday.

Nancy and I had a few free hours, so we went into town for a date. I know she has talked of other things besides the Mexican food she ate in the states, but I don't recall anything except that.

I was craving Mexican food, and we found a Mexican restaurant!!

I don't want to alarm anyone, but based on the food we ate, the only scientific conclusion I can draw is this:

Africa is whiter than Indiana.

I didn't know that was possible.

When you have twins, people assume that they do things in a similar manner, and it must be all sorts of cute. For whatever reason, our twins seem to do opposite things in similar situations.

Take for instance the mirror. After I bathe a baby, I dry them near a mirror. Ben will take a cursory look, probably looking for food or toys that he can dismantle. Once he sees they aren't there, he isn't much interested.

Katie, on the other hand, beams her brightest smile at the mirror, as if to say `I'm SO glad there are other quality people here BESIDES me.' She has remained generally fascinated by her reflection.

I have a little song I sing to them that goes "Who's my favorite boy/girl in the whole wide world. It's you, it's you." When I sing `you' I touch their noses. Katie flashes a brilliant smile. Ben uses it as an opportunity to stick his finger far far into the upper reaches of his nose.

The only thing I see that they both do is that before a bath, after I remove their clothes, both like to loudly pat their tummies. As with many things with the twins, I don't know what this signifies.

The process of adoption has slowly begun. We had to have one more home visit by the social worker, who came when Nancy was still in America. I had fears of both children raging, but they were on their most charming behavior.

She did ask JT and Matthew what they thought about having a black brother and sister. Matthew said that he loved them because they were his brother and sister. She asked if when we went back to the states, what would they think if children teased them because of the color of their skin. JT said he didn't think that would happen, but it wouldn't change the way he felt about the babies. The social worker told us she would recommend us to the courts.

Last week we met with the attorney. She confirmed to us that since the law was changed in March, no one knows how to interpret it, so most courts have not heard any adoption cases. Our friends who were here last school year were granted a miracle in their adoption, but there have been very few miracles lately.

We were grateful that it would be one cost, not two, but even at that, the adoption will cost more than a month's salary for us. All I could think of is how many babies need to be adopted, and on the $25 dollar a month the average Kenyan makes, how adoption would be impossible for so many of them.

The bad news that we got was that the adoption would probably not proceed until next year. The problem with that is that the elections are supposed to be in December, and there is some fear that the country will experience some turmoil. We want the adoption to be finalized so we can get out with them if we need to.

In Congo this week, all the AIM missionaries were ordered evacuated, because of the civil war there. We hope it doesn't happen here, but last week Kenya was named one of the top ten most corrupt nations in the world. We're just not sure what will happen.

The one thing we are sure of is that we picked names for the twins. For the first time, may I present Katherine Izawadi Peifer and Benjamin Ikhavi Peifer. The middle names are from the Luhya tribe, which they are from. Izawadi means gift, and Ikhavi means blessing.

What a gift, and what a blessing they have been.

Your pal,

Steve

Wheelchairs Aren't Funny; It Just SEEMED That Way
— September 23, 2002

Grace told our Swahili teacher that he should bring Nancy a present for how well she is doing in language studies. It seemed natural to ask her `Don't you think he should bring ME a present also?'

At this point, something happened that was difficult to interpret culturally. Fortunately, I have been in Africa for a while and have developed an expertise to interpret what occurred next.

Grace started laughing as hard as I have ever seen anyone laugh. She went to another friend and told her what I had said, and they both laughed so much that I thought they might become ill. My interpretation is that my language skills are SO high that it would be impossible to find an appropriate gift, and the thought of searching for such a gift amused them greatly.

I can't think of any other logical explanation.

Kijabe, where we live, is very hilly.

One of my best friends here, Greg, is a large 6'6 guy. He is one of those guys who is good at everything (computer guru, biology teacher, etc etc etc) and who is always calm and helpful.

He recently had surgery on both feet. He asked me to pick him up from the hospital. But it was another example of how Kenya is a bit different than the US.

He had been given a shot to deaden the pain, and it wasn't enough, so they gave him another whole shot. This rendered him quite incoherent, and very groggy.

When his wife and I arrived at the hospital, he was laying in a bed in a room with 12 other patients, all waiting to be picked up to leave. He was still in his hospital gown, and we were told to go in the hallway so he could change. We managed to get him into the wheelchair and I gathered his clothes and went to the secluded hallway.

It was all Greg could do to stand up, and being fairly out of it, he dropped trou right in front of me. There was a point in my life when I thought I was a mooning magnet, but I did not expect it to occur in Africa. After a fairly lengthy struggle, we got his clothes on and he got back into the wheelchair.

The hospital is built on a hilly area, and so there were many ramps to go up. This was not a high quality wheelchair, and it was hard to push it. I went up the first ramp, got almost to the top, and we slid back down. I started running the second time, and his wife started pushing, and we made it up the first ramp.

By the time I saw the next ramp I started laughing. There was no way I was going to be able to get him up that ramp. I started running and we hit a bad section of the floor, and all I could think about was that poor Greg was going to have to crawl home, because he almost fell out of the chair. However, with the help of another guy, we made it to the door.

Doors and wheelchairs and guys with foot surgeries shouldn't be funny, but I didn't know if I could stop laughing as I tried to figure out how to open the door without using his injured feet to do it. At this point, I'm sure Greg felt he was being punished for something he had done previously and his punishment was me pushing him.

After a good bit of time, I got Greg into the car, and we drove to his house. It was then I realized that the adventure was just beginning. His wife had stayed behind to pay the bill (that can take hours at a Kenyan hospital), and they live on the highest point on the campus, and he was so drugged up that he fell asleep during the five-minute drive to his house.

I drove as close as I could to the house, but we would still have to walk up at least 15 stairs together. After I woke him up, we began; Greg a large 6'6 and me a rather meager 5'11. We got up two stairs with great effort and much leaning and then he said:

> Greg: Do you think there is another way we could do this?
>
> Me: What do you mean?
>
> Greg: I'm not sure I want to go up any more steps.
>
> Me: (increasingly desperate with Greg leaning on me) I'm not sure we have many options right now Greg.
>
> Greg: I just think there might be a better way to do this.
>
> Me: There isn't!! We've got to move!! Go Greg Go!!

At this point, with Greg leaning on me and looking like he was going to fall asleep, I did not show myself a great leader of man. There was nothing funny about what was going on, but I started laughing. It seemed to wake Greg up. With much coaxing and straining, I got him to the house and his bed, where he slept for most of the day. He doesn't remember how he got home.

I'll never forget.

But I wonder what happened to all the other people waiting with no one with a car to help them get home. It was hard for us; I can't imagine what they do.

Your pal,

Steve

P.S. All the Kenyan schoolteachers on our strike, so there is no feeding going on right now. There have been threats by the President to hire replacement teachers, and threats by the striking teachers that they will murder any replacement teachers that come to teach. There have been several reported deaths so far, so we are laying low until the smoke clears. It looks like we will be able to add several schools in January, and we are grateful for the support. I was told that enrollments increased, and one headmaster told me it was because of the lunch program. Thank you for what you are doing.

Feet Greetings
— October 9, 2002

I'm 47, and I'm not sure I've every had a real thought about jellybeans. In the states, I might eat some when they are around, but I don't remember ever buying them and I don't particularly enjoy them.

Nancy brought some back from the states, and Sunday night we opened the bag. It was one of those with many different kinds of flavors, and we spent over an hour, going around in a circle, choosing and eating them one by one.

Each choice was agonized over, and much discussion occurred over each jellybean. (Is that cherry or red pepper? Was the blueberry worthy of seconds?)

It was so much fun. Scarcity does have its advantages.

Someone had a double stroller that they sold us, and Ben and Katie enjoy being pushed around campus. If they spot you, they respond with huge grins, but the best part is that two pairs of legs start waving as fast and hard as they can. I can't recall a better greeting.

This has been a tough week in many ways, and an example of how tough things can lead to a better place. One of our dorm guys was caught doing something he shouldn't have been doing by one of his teachers, and it was very embarrassing for him. He spent many hours weeping in the teacher's office as the teacher tried to explain that he was forgiven and that everyone made mistakes.

He would have little of that, and was beating himself us pretty badly. That night, he asked me for help with his bible homework. He asked me what the scripture meant that said `The Lord does not require sacrifice, but a broken and contrite spirit.'

It's hard to distinguish between doing good things for God and being broken in your spirit when you are in eighth grade, but when I told him `what happened to you today could be an example of someone who has a contrite heart, or someone who will change a behavior so he won't be caught. A contrite heart will move beyond right and wrong to doing something out of love. What happened to you today?'

His tears were an indication that something good was happening. The week continued with an annual event at RVA called Spiritual Emphasis Week, where a special speaker is brought in and there are several meetings with him/her.

This year the speaker was particularly gifted and challenging, and the kids responded to his message in a wonderfully positive way. One night he encouraged kids to make sure they didn't have any issues with each other, and much of the evening kids were making things right with each other.

I got involved with it because several students came up to me and told me in so many words that they had never liked me and felt like they needed to apologize and ask my forgiveness. The reason they gave was my insensitivity and sarcasm.

I'm sure those of you that have read many of these know I can be an insensitive clod, and young children are particularly vulnerable to being teased. It's been my mode of operation for as long as I can remember, but I really was convicted as to how I can use humor in so many wrong ways: as a habit, as a weapon, as a shield, and as a way to relate to people instead of really relating to people.

Humor has it's place, and I don't want to become boring, but there is a balance, and I'm at that wonderful place where I know I need to change and I don't have a clue as to how to change. It's both painful and exciting, and I would ask your prayers.

I've saved the best for last. One of our dorm boys is an Indian Muslim named Rahim. He is a wonderful boy, full of life and adventure, and we have really grown to love him and his family. They invited us to their home a few weeks ago for a meal, and it was a wonderful time of getting to know them.

Today Rahim made a decision to become a Christian. After one of the meetings last week, he told me that he was thinking hard about Christianity. What I really appreciated was that it wasn't an emotional decision. Two of the guys in the dorm cautioned him about his decision, and encouraged him to count the costs involved. He asked lots and lots of good questions, and he was really trying to figure it out.

I believe there is an empty spot in all of us that can only be filled with Jesus Christ, and if you could see Rahim today, you would see a different person than was there yesterday.

We are so grateful.

The strike continues, the political unrest is becoming more violent, we are beginning to be encouraged to do some stock up buying because we're not sure it will be safe to go into town anymore, but in the midst of it all, we have seen His hand move, and we are so grateful.

Your pal,

Steve

A Kiss Is Still A Kiss (Giraffes Excepted)
— *October 18, 2002*

We haven't done to many outings with the babies yet. When you take two naps a day, and most things are an hour away, it tends to cramp your style. But we are now in the land of one nap a day, so the six of us went to the Giraffe Center in Nairobi.

Things are more relaxed in Africa. There was hardly anything separating the giraffes from us. The giraffes would eat out of your hand. They would even eat out of your MOUTH, if you were foolish enough to let them.

I'm sure that many of you are asking the question `What was it like to kiss a giraffe, Steve.' All I can tell you is that giraffes have NO future in a kissing booth. But the thrill was actually being able to gross out my older children, who did NOT relish the tables being reversed.

Both babies are at a wonderful stage where they will sit and sing. Ben really only has one word, so his songs tend to be `Da Da Da Da' which of course I enjoy. Katie is so verbal that Nancy believes that when she actually begins talking, the rest of us will never get another chance. But on the way home, one would fall asleep and the other would sing. One of the fun things about having older and younger kids is that the older ones will ask ` Did I do that?' and you remember sweet things you hadn't thought about in years.

We had a dorm night on Friday. We went down to the lower field and played `Capture the Flag' built a huge bonfire and roasted hot dogs and marshmallows. You really haven't played `capture the flag' until you've played in Africa; pitch black adds a different dimension. After two games in the dark, we ate and then the guys would take branches heated in the fire and run down the field with them. Some of them had battles and it had a `Star Wars' light saber look to it.

As I watched the 16 8th grade boys just have such a time with the fire, I reflected how wonderful it was and that perhaps the greatest gift Africa is to my older children is that it has allowed them to remain children a little bit longer than they might be able to in the United States. Without TV and Internet, there is not quite the push here to have a girl friend or be cool like in the US.

As the evening ended, one of the guys asked if we could go annoy the girl's dorm. The rest of the guys said no, and I thought: it won't be long before all that starts, but how nice to be in junior high and still be a kid.

As I pondered those warm thoughts, one guy yelled `We've got to put out the fire!" Another yelled `Drink all the water you can!' And as I realized what they intended to do, all my warm thoughts were extinguished, if you know what I mean.

Childhood is great, but there is something to be said for growing up, too.

Your pal,

Steve

PS. They expected riots in Nairobi on Monday during nominations of one of the major parties, but a huge group left that party and so it was a peaceful day. Does this mean that the general election will be tumultuous? No one knows, but we are grateful for the peaceful day we had.

Baby Break Out!
— *October 31, 2002*

Sunday morning, I went next door to borrow something. Nancy went into the bedroom to put on her shoes. The babies were playing in the living room.

We came back, and the babies were gone. They are usually in the living room, where a barrier and closed door keeps them confined. But they had gotten out. We searched through the house, and couldn't find them anywhere.

Finally, we went out the back door. There, in the pouring rain, sat our two babies, dressed in their Sunday finest, in the largest mud puddle they could find, splashing and laughing. They were having such a big time you couldn't help but enjoy it, although during the bath to clean them off, it was easy to forget enjoying it.

This was a big day, because our dorm asked the eighth grade GIRLS dorm to come over and watch a movie. Some of our of guys were thrilled, and several tried to hide in their bedrooms because they were so nervous. Being a dorm parent of eighth grade guys has convinced me that I am VERY glad I don't have to relive that part of my life, but I think they all had a big time.

Eighth grade is such a weird year; some of the girls looked like they could date the Dallas Cowboys, and eighth grade guys look like eighth grade guys. Someday the inequities will even out, but right now I have to tell some of them `your day will come.'

The four-week teacher strike is over, and Kenyan children are finally back at school. One of them told a pastor that she was glad the strike was over because she was hungry. We are excited that the feeding continues and we will be able to add two schools in January.

The election is scheduled for December 27th, and it really will be interesting to see what happens. So far, there are obvious tensions but no real violence. We are grateful for that, and we are hoping for good things.

This week was a time of real contrasts, and somehow it explains to me why Kenya has the problems it has. I was invited to a harambe for a pastor. A harambe is when the entire community unites to help someone out. It is a good thing in principle, but too often it replaces good stewardship in Africa. And then when you are asked time after time after time you start to get numb to it all.

This pastor is a good friend of mine, and we have had many adventures together with the orphanage and the school lunch program. If you saw the car he drove, you would know that he is not living high on the hog. He is almost 60, and has worked hard his whole life.

But the harambe was to send him to England for a refreshing vacation. And he had pretty high expectations that the missionaries would pay for a good part of it.

The bottom line is that I can't really understand the bone crunching poverty of Africa, and he doesn't understand that when I was in the states and made a six-figure income, it never occurred to me to take an international vacation because I couldn't afford it. Now I make a tenth of that, but I am so rich compared to most Kenyans that they don't see the limit to our money, and ask things that might be inappropriate.

But is it inappropriate? He has worked so hard, and without a break for so many years, that is it unreasonable to have one big vacation? In the United States, we've given money to send our pastor on much needed vacations. Why is this different?

How do you deal with that in the context of hunger and children not being in school because they don't have the school fees?

I really don't know the answer, but I suspect that some of Kenya's issues are people overreaching instead of dealing with the greatest needs. How you prioritize is a hard question for any of us; in Africa, it can often be a life and death question.

In the same week, our friend Joel's wife had a baby, and we had offered to have a baby bed made for him when he told me that most Africans can't afford to have a separate bed for their babies, so they sleep on the floor. Joel is the man who borrowed (and repaid) the money for his famous cow `Kowjabe.' So I went to his house to deliver the bed.

Joel lives almost four miles away. It can take him over ninety minutes to walk to work. He and his wife live in a home with walls of mud and canvas grain bags on the walls to keep the rain out. They have a dirt floor, no windows and cook over an open flame.

We put the crib in the house, and it almost didn't fit because it was so large compared to the rest of the house. Most Kenyan babies don't have a bed; it just boggles my western mind.

So, in the same week, I'm involved in helping someone take a vacation and giving a baby a bed.

When there are limited resources, you've got to make the right choice. Those choices are hard ones, and I think that is the biggest issue in Africa today.

In the same way, it is an issue for all of us. How do we prioritize what is important? If someone doesn't do that carefully out here, they usually die. Sometimes I wish I could view my resources in that context; that how I spend my money can make the difference between life and death.

I wish I could conclude this with nice homilies, but Africa is way beyond easy answers for me.

Steve

Oh, It's Ok; I've Been Poisoned Before
— *November 6, 2002*

A great former missionary, the invincible Doug Dempsey, once told me `It's not if, it's when.' The great scourge of all African missionaries, it strikes without warning. Whether it is the water, food that has gone south, or something in the air, it struck without warning, but much subsequent fanfare.

We had SIXTY-ONE kids in the infirmary with food poisoning on Friday. When you have a campus of five hundred kids, that means there was a LOT of sudden running. It also led to two of the greatest quotes I've heard in awhile.

Me: How are you doing?

Them1: Oh, it's ok. I've been poisoned before.

Me: How about you? How are you feeling?

Them2: It was the chicken.

Me: How do you know?

Them2: My upper stomach hurts. If it hurt lower, it would be the milk.

The most inspiring part of all of it was that the more CREATIVE students started to see the trend, and they suddenly began to complain about great pains especially before a class with a test. There is nothing like seeing someone clutch the right part of their stomach, and minutes later be clutching their left side, to stir the voting members of the Academy to judge great performances. Truly inspirational, especially when recovery occurred in time for soccer practice.

We gave the SAT test on Saturday. The whole college thing is so stressful for all high school kids, but these kids have parents whose income would be considered poverty level in the United States, and high scores that produce scholarships are the best, and sometimes, the only shot they have to go to a good school.

There is one company in the whole of Kenya who handles the test, and the manager told us she would pick up the tests on Monday. She came out to campus on Monday, we greeted her, and she took the tests and drove off.

The problem was: she got carjacked right outside the campus. Six men, two with guns, forced her out and took off in the car.

She was badly frightened, but not hurt, and her car was recovered because they couldn't figure out how to drive it. We were so grateful she was ok.

And the tests were not damaged. SAT is a rather anal type of company; I'm not sure how we would have explained that the tests were kidnapped.

We just got word that a family from RVA was in a head on collusion with a truck, and one of the children may be in serious condition. His name is Paul; will you pray for him?

Your pal,

Steve

Eggactly My Point
— *November 19, 2002*

After the fiasco with the babies escaping through the back door and playing in the rain and the largest puddles they could find, we identified the culprit (the dog) who pushed the doors open for them. We changed the ways the door closed so it couldn't happen again.

So Nancy took the babies for a walk, and the egg man came and dropped off some eggs in our `safe' room. They were on the shelf, and Nancy didn't notice them when she returned and placed the babies in the room and walked into the kitchen.

The babies noticed them, and instantly went to work. In less than two minutes, they had tested almost every egg, and found them to be structurally unsound. We didn't get pictures of this one; it was too messy, but funnier as time went on.

This morning, Nancy was in the kitchen and noticed a different sound from Katie. She had managed to get on top of the piano, and was sitting on the keyboard. I think the next year will be FULL of adventures.

African skin has surprised me, but African hair has been a true revelation. All of the woman reading this can just shake their heads and include me on the clueless list, but I had no idea how hair extensions worked. I just sort of figured that someone hair grew long or something; I didn't know.

It is quite common for African woman to use hair extensions to style their hair. There is a woman who lives nearby who offered to come over and do it. The result was: rage from Katie who didn't want to sit still for two hours and tears from me who didn't want to see his baby girl look like a grown up woman.

She really does look cute, but they are fascinating to Ben, who enjoys pulling them off, which gives her a unique look. I'm going to try to learn how to do extensions and braids, but I had to leave the room while they were doing it; this business of being a dad to a girl is going to be more challenging than I thought.

Some friends had a brief layover in Nairobi, so we went into town to see them. On the way back, the main road was covered with thousands of people attending a political rally. If 635 in Dallas or the Dan Ryan Expressway in Chicago were closed due to a political rally, it would be a shock, but apparently it is quite common here. It was scary, and we were driving through at five miles an hour, but all we got were waves and smiles. Kenyan elections can easily turn violent, so we were grateful to get through with no problems.

The major cause of death of missionaries in Kenya is auto accidents, and last week was an example of what can happen out here. Some friends were driving into town, and on their way back, a bus blew a tire and hit them head on. The driver broke his hand, the rest of the passengers were bruised, but 13 year old Paul broke both legs, both wrists, and has suffered head trauma. The full extents of his injuries aren't known yet. I saw a picture of the tire of the truck that blew; absolutely no thread.

Paul is slowly recovering, and we are grateful that he is alive. If you saw the car, you wouldn't think anyone was alive who was in it, but He extended His mercies once again.

Another thing struck me about this incident. Paul had a tough week prior to the accident. He had some discipline issues that were difficult, and I imagine that it would have been easy to have words at their home.

But we never know how much time we have. I want to make sure my words are appropriate, because you never know if they will be the last words you get a chance to say.

I want to always try to end on a good note. You never know.

Your pal,

Steve

Unhappy Coincidence
— *December 1, 2002*

You can tell when the end of the term is because the children start playing Christmas music rather early getting ready for the end of term Christmas concert. The older kids do a wonderful job, but the concert of the younger kids' band is a marvel to behold. Many of them have had instruments for just a few months, and the sounds they make are fascinating.

I've learned that you should NEVER make eye contact with another adult during one of the performances. The fifth and sixth graders performed Jingle Bells, and I'm sure you could have gotten a similar sound by taking a large stick and whacking a big cow. At one point, during an unsuccessful stretch for a note, I made the mistake of looking at a staff member who was trying valiantly to not laugh, which made keeping a lid on it pretty tough, but the wonders of being married almost 18 years is that she knows me well, and her elbows helped me contain myself.

Right after school gets out, there is a conference for all the missionaries in the area at RVA. Many of these folks are way out in the bush, and the stories they tell are remarkable. One told of their daughter being asked by a Masai tribe to go zebra hunting. The males pride themselves in their hunting skills, and Masai woman never hunt. They asked her as a joke, and she took one bullet to get her zebra. To celebrate and honor her, they allowed her to wash her face in the zebra's blood.

Another missionary is a 70-year-old force of nature who goes into Sudan, probably the most dangerous place in Africa to be in. She has been shot at and had to flee from bombings as she goes in to help. Nothing deters her; she keeps going back because of her love for the people.

I thought about this as I stuffed envelopes this week. I'm working in the Guidance office, and had the misfortune to replace someone who was not only the coolest person on the campus, but also had done the job for years and knew it inside and out. I've not yet had a cool day in my life, and I am learning as I am going.

God uses everything that we've done, or at least He has out here. I had a job once where I traveled to colleges, and had the opportunity to visit almost 800 campuses. So I have been able to bring a little perspective to the kids as they try to make their college decisions.

As far as we have been able to tell, the kids have responded well to my talking about colleges. So well that we have had about five times the normal applications from the kids at RVA. Because of where most of their families live, it is our job to process the applications and get them ready to be mailed. It is also our job to find people returning to the states who will take mail, because the Kenyan post office is not too safe or reliable.

What it has meant for me in the past ten days is working 12 hours a day trying to get applications done. As I've listened to the cool stories of missionaries who are doing astonishing things, the later it got, the more I tended to wish I were doing something cool instead.

It hasn't happened often to me, but this was a time when I think I received a revelation. Probably obvious to most of you, but it really was made clear to me that in life, it's not what we do, but why and how we do it. As I contemplated that, I repented of my lousy attitude and tried to do it unto Him. It's not a glamorous job, but I know it is what I'm supposed to be doing right now. And if I'm doing what I've been called to do, and doing it with a good heart, it will bear good fruit.

I don't know if you've ever had the experience of reading a newspaper and learning that the plane you were going to be on tomorrow crashed. On Friday, we learned of the bombing in Mombassa.

On the sixth, we were scheduled to fly to Mombassa. We aren't being foolish; we are staying in a modest villa far away from the fancy tourist resorts there It was an unsettling coincidence, but one that reaffirmed to us that our safety is in His hands.

It became more clear when Paul, the boy hurt in the car wreck, was allowed to go home. He has months and months of recovery ahead of him, but it is a miracle that he is still alive.

It goes back to this: the safest place to be is where He wants you to be.

Your pal,

Steve

Hitting Crocodiles on the Head – Vacations in Africa
— *December 17, 2002*

We had a lovely restful peaceful vacation in Mombassa last week. The absolute great thing about Africa is that it never seems to stop throwing curveballs at you. Near the place where we stayed was a small reptile zoo, so we stopped in.

The first surprise was that we were the only people there. The guy at the front told me the price he wanted me to pay, which was much more than I had expected, and more than the posted sign. I said no, and so he changed the price. I wondered what that would do for Disneyland to negotiate your price when you entered.

The guy that took our money also gave us a tour. The first stop was the place where they had several crocodiles. I've been to the zoo so many times, and I've never seen a crock do anything. But I was now in an African zoo, and so the first surprise started.

Animals in zoos in America are treated with a great deal of love an d respect. It's a little different here. The guy grabbed a long stick and whacked the crock on the head. He did it again, and the crock hissed like you might expect a dragon to hiss if there were dragons. Then he hit him on the back so the crock would swirl around.

He then told us to come to the python pit. He then jumped IN the pit. He grabbed a 9-foot python by the head and pulled it over his head. He then appeared to stroke the python on the head, which caused the python to open his mouth is a way that made me jump high in the air, even while I was holding Katie.

The next few exhibits were behind glass. There were many signs explaining how poisonous the snakes were, and how rapidly we would die if we were bitten. But at least two of the cages had deep cuts in the glass. For that matter, Bill B. and I built a fort when we were in 5th grade, and put in one piece of glass, and I promise you, our glass looked more professional than cages holding very deadly snakes.

After we left, we sought the refuge of the ocean. Because we are residents and therefore qualified for a big discount, we were able to give JT an early Christmas present: he would get certified to scuba dive. It began auspiciously for him: a snake fell from the ceiling and crawled angrily out of the room during his first class.

After the first dive in a pool, they had to have four dives in the ocean. On the first dive, he was a foot away from a twenty foot whale shark. They are as harmless as 20foot things can be, but it was fantastic to see something like that on your first dive.

They warned him that not every dive would have sights so astonishing. So, on the second dive, after seeing dozens of different fish, including several sea turtles that were huge, they were 2 feet away from a 24-foot whale shark. My children have seen some of the roughest things on earth; people going without food, children whose parents died of aids, and all the strange medical problems that seem to afflict people here.

I'm so glad that they get to see some other sights also.

Your pal,

Steve

You Have Saved Us From The Choice
— *December 27, 2002*

Besides the obvious holiday, we celebrated our first year with the babies on December 23. It would be hard to name highlights: it was harder than I thought it would be, and more fun than I imagined it could be. Any babies at my age would be a challenge: twins at my age exposed all the selfishness that I continue to harbor in my heart. The most amazing part of it all is this: They were not part of our family, and now we can't imagine life without them.

After a wonderful Christmas, we celebrated a peaceful election. No one was expecting this, and we are grateful for so many who were praying. Many Kenyans have called this a peaceful coup. We prefer to call it democracy. It is a thrill to see how excited Kenyans are about a change, and it is becoming evident to them that if this group doesn't do what they promised, they can be thrown out also.

The results of the first three months of the school lunch program have been nothing short of miraculous. The usual drop out rate hovers at about 30-35%. At the first two schools we provided lunches for (Kamuyu and Nyakinyua), not one student dropped out. Not one. At the third school, Namuncha, one student dropped out, and that was because his father died of AIDS and his mother needed him at home. We were hoping for good results, but this is far greater than we dreamed of.

We have been able to add two more schools to the three we already provide lunches for as of the first of the year: Karima and Rare. Karima has almost 600 students and Rare has 100. We haven't seen Rare yet. This past Thursday when we delivered food for the next school term, we had almost 40,000 pounds or 20 TONS of grain and maize in the truck, and it got stuck in the non-road. We were there for several hours until it dried up enough for me to pull it out with my Land Cruiser.

As we were digging and getting rocks to try to provide traction, I marveled that I wasn't upset. Something always goes wrong when I deliver the maize and beans. It used to drive me nuts; now I understand that things just happen in Africa. As I was hauling rocks, one Kenyan man came by to help (which in itself was amazing; we were in the middle of nowhere) and he had a small radio in his pocket. As we were chatting, all of a sudden `This Kiss' by Faith Hill began playing on his radio. I couldn't help but laugh, and marvel at a God who would play a country and western song for me in the middle of Kenya.

Several parents heard we were coming and showed up to say thank you to you all. One father told me that this was the first time in his child's life that she ate two meals in the same day. Another father thanked you all because you had given his children a chance. Another said he had hope again.

Another mother told me to thank the people who saved her from the `choice.' I asked her what the choice was. She said the choice is when you decide if you feed your children or send them to school. Because of this program, she didn't have to make the choice.

Our children's school in the states gave us some money to buy beds for a local orphanage, and we are going to be able to buy almost 100 beds. I told the pastor, and he just sat and cried. They use cheap foam mattresses, and most of them are over 5 years old and in great disrepair.

To be able to be the one to give food to hungry children or purchase beds for orphans is a dream come true; a dream I didn't even know I had until I got here. Thank you for helping us be here, and for blessing the children.

For almost two thousand children, you have saved them from the choice

Your pal,

Steve

Letters from 2003

No, The Black One
— *January 20, 2003*

Kenya has changed its laws, and to adopt, the courts appoint a guardian from the Kenyan Child Welfare Society to oversee how you raise the children. She was scheduled to come to our home, but at the last moment she asked us to come to her office. For those of you old enough to remember the old Batman show, her office looked like an abandoned factory now used for nefarious means by criminal masterminds. It was scary to go inside, and there was no signage anywhere, so we had to knock on closed doors to find where we were supposed to go.

We finally found it, and as we looked around at the dilapidated office, with broken windows and holes in the floor, it was hard to imagine what would happen next. After two hours past our appointment time, a very nice woman came and talked with us for an hour. She then said that she would come and do a home visit in the next week.

The following week she came, and we had a very nice visit. There was somewhere nearby who she needed to visit, so afterwards, Nancy drove her to that home. When she got out of the car, she saw a large dog coming at her. She is a large woman who has had a bad experience with a dog, so her response was to jump on Nancy's foot and duck behind her. The dog was harmless, and Nancy only got a slight bruise, but she might now forget the experience for a while. The next step is court; we hope that will be soon.

I went to Nyakinyua today to help prepare the lunches and see how the program is going. Kenya has declared free education for all primary school students, which has caused a huge increase in the amount of students attending. The schools have been set up to accept tuition, and have received no monies as yet from the government, so it will be interesting to see how this all plays out. At several schools, the amount of students has tripled. Nyakinyua has seen an increase of almost 100 children.

I was trying to find the headmaster, and although other friends of mine have had similar conversations, I never thought it would happen to me:

Me: Where is the headmaster?
Them: Just there.
Me: Which one? That one?
Them: No, the black one.

At this point I must point out that I was the only white person for 20 miles.

Me: They all look black to me.

Them: They are brown! He is the black one!

I found him (he WAS blacker) and we went to prepare the food. They had three big pots cooking the maize and beans, and empty butter containers for the children plates. They had no forks or spoons; everyone ate by hand.

If you have ever seen five hundred children eat maize and beans with their hands like they have never eaten before, it is as sobering an experience as you will ever experience on this planet.

Your Pal,

Steve

Asst

— *January 25, 2003*

Eighth grades guys can go from awkward to slick in moments. One of our dorm boys, fearing that we would tease him, would ask if he could call his sister. We would say yes, and he would call her and ask `Can I have all your money?' She would hang up, and then he would call the eighth grade girl he really wanted to talk to.

We have short devotions in the dorm Monday through Thursday, and because they get really sick of me, I ask them who they want to come do guest devotion. They used to ask for the senior guys who are the soccer stars; now they ask for cute senior girls. At the end, I ask one of our guys to escort her home. Afterwards, the guys hover around the one who escorted the senior girl and drill him about their conversation:

Them: What did you talk about?

Him: Nothing.

Them: You're lying! (Sounds of fists)

Him: I asked her if she liked the meatloaf in the cafeteria.

Them: (in frantic tones) WHAT DID SHE SAY? WHAT DID SHE SAY?

Him: She said it was ok.

Them: UNBELIEVABLE! SHE SAID IT WAS OK!

I am very glad I am no longer an eighth grade guy and even gladder that I'm not a senior girl at this school. Weird adoration would get really old. fast.

I have a problem I need help with. In the main office, they have a little bulletin board with the staff names and titles. It goes like this:

Jim Long	Superintendent
Mark Kinzer	Dean of Students
Tim Hall	Principal
Mark Buhler	Director of Guidance
Steve Peifer	Asst

I've never been a title guy, but this needs work. So, I am announcing my second annual contest. Some of you might remember the ferocious competition to name a cow last year. This year: suggest a title for me that the administration will accept, and the winner will receive a Masai leather beaded belt in your size!

The rules are simple. Entries must be in by Feb 2 via email. In case of identical names, first one here wins. And the most important rule is this: the true wits among you who think that adding `BIG' or `DUMB' in front of my present title are NOT FUNNY.

I've had two detached retinas, so I have to get them checked every year. I went to Nairobi to see the laser surgeon because while Kijabe has some excellent doctors, they don't have any eye surgeons. After the doctor looked at my eyes, he asked me the following questions:

Him: What is this Claritin?

Me: It is a prescription allergy medicine.

Him: How often do you take it?

Me: Daily.

Him: You are addicted.

Me: I've never had an eye doctor comment on allergy medicine before.

Him: And you need extensive surgery.

I haven't been having any eye issues, but I knew at this point I didn't have warm fuzzies with him. I started looking at making the trek to go back to the states to have my eyes checked but never got serious because of the price.

Then, an old friend asked me if I was planning on attending our 30th high school reunion in July. I had heard about it, but never thought about attending. He then said he wasn't going to go if I didn't go, so would I be interested in a ticket from him? (Nancy says he is the nicest guy in the world; my theory is that although he is nice, he wanted the security of someone who is guaranteed to be fatter and balder than he is)

Long story short, thanks to the kindness of an old friend; I will be in the United States for three weeks this summer. I will arrive on July 15th in Chicago, go to Texas on July 21st to have the eyes checked, and leave for Africa on August 4. If there is a way to get together, I'll find a way to make it happen. If I can't see you, I want to at least call you and say hi and hear voices! And, if your church is looking for an exciting missionary to speak to them, I know several I can recommend. But if that doesn't work, I would be thrilled if you settled for me.

See you soon, and save some Mexican food for me.

Your pal,

Steve

Your Pal, Steve

I Have Unwittingly Become A Member Of The Communist Party

— January 31, 2003

You change when you have been out here for a while. We had a monkey come into our house last week, and while it was a thrill (and more of a thrill that he didn't hang around, because monkeys celebrate coming into homes by pooping in them) I see them quite often and wasn't totally shocked.

But this is the big one. I didn't know that the Super bowl was last weekend. What kind of American can I be if I don't follow the Super bowl? I've racked my brain, and the only conclusion a rational man can come to is this:

Somehow, I have unwittingly become a member of the communist party.

I never thought it would happen to me. A kind friend is sending me a copy, and I promise to watch it as soon as I get it just to become an American again, but it is pretty darn scary.

Some parts of Africa are exciting and good, like monkeys, and some are scary. We have had a rash of carjackings lately, and while no one has been seriously hurt, they have struck a good friend with a rangu. A rungu is a stick with a wooden knob on the end; it would hurt. The friends who were carjacked 10 days ago noticed at the end that the thugs had wooden guns, but by then it was too late.

Last weekend, Rahim, one of our dorm boys who has just recently become a Christian, ran into the kitchen to tell me that his parents had been attacked on their way up to campus. They were able to get away, but there was lots of damage to the car, and his little sister was just sobbing when I got there.

One of the saddest parts of all of this is that they caught the guys once, but within two hours, they were released from prison. Most of the people in prison in Africa are there because they can't pay the bribe it would take to get out. It looks like they have been apprehended again; maybe that will end the unease we all feel right now.

The saddest thing of all is that the first family they attacked does so much good for the community. He is a physical therapist, and he does clinics all over Kenya all the time. He's not the guy you want afraid to go out; he is the only therapist that most kids in the bush will ever see.

I went to Karima this week. It is the largest school we are supporting, and one of the poorest. Because they are offering free education up to 6th grade, they have 200 more children then they are equipped to handle, and many children are sitting on the dirt floors of the crowded classrooms.

So many of the children thanked me, and I told them it wasn't from me, it was from friends in the states. I brought some names and asked if they wanted to write some thank yous, and the headmaster told me that they didn't have any paper for that. Next time I will bring paper, but it was another reminder of what they go through. Imagine running a school with no paper for children to write on.

I'm saving the best for last. We've had lots of extraordinary things happen to us since we've been in Africa, but this has got to go to the top of the list.

We've been trying to get a court date to adopt for eight months now, and we finally were assigned one. We were so thrilled to finally get a date that we didn't even realize the significance of the date until several hours later.

Many of you know that we had a son who would have been five this year. Stephen only lived a few days, and his life and death changed us forever. He was born on March 4th.

Which is the day we go to court to adopt the babies.

When we realized what had happened, it took our breath away. March 4th has always been a tough day, but besides sad memories, it will now also hold a new beginning.

I love how God can redeem the unredeemable.

Your pal,

Steve

The Greatest Fear
— *February 8, 2003*

There are always interesting parts of living in a dorm, but perhaps the most highly anticipated is Korean food day, or as it is always referred to `delicious Korean food day.' All of the Korean parents come to campus and cook tremendous amounts of Korean food.

Before I go on, let me point out that I really like Korean food. When Nancy went back to the states last summer and asked what I wanted brought back, the first thing I thought of was seaweed, which my Korean dorm boys have gotten me addicted to. I think Korean food is wonderful.

However, since my Korean guys only get this delicacy once a year, they feel a moral obligation to eat beyond any reasonable limit. This produces so much methane that I fear a smoker will enter the dorm after Korean food day and they whole campus will be destroyed in an atomic fireball.

When I go from room to room to say goodnight, they have gotten in the habit of asking me to rate the odor level of the room. Being eighth grade guys, it is a point of pride to be rated the smelliest. There are five rooms in the dorm, and I would say that it is an absolute tie right now.

The greatest fear of a dorm kid is that a family member will be hurt when he is away from them. That fear came true this week for one of our dorm guys. Joey is one of the nicest kids you could ever meet in your life, and a smile that could chase away the rain. His brother Justin, who is 16, was home with his parents in Zambia when he passed away in his sleep.

You always feel inadequate as a dorm parent; if the truth be known, I often feel inadequate as a parent, but never so much as when we got the news. Imagine being 14 and having to handle that without your parents. We all cried and cried, and then we had to tell the dorm.

Joey is pretty universally loved her, and so the dorm cried and cried. Those who had suffered sibling lost took it the worst, and I was surprised how many of them there were. In eighth grade, everyone tends to take everything personally, and most things become `what if this happens to me?' It was a very sad, very troubled night.

Joey was able to go home, although it was a six-hour plan ride and then an all day car ride from there. His parents live in a very remote part of Africa. There can't be too many things harder than what they are going through; please pray for them as they come to mind. Joey's brother and sister are going to college in the states, and finances are preventing them from coming back to the funeral. That has just got to be such a tough situation for all of them.

Back in the dorm, things were pretty tentative for a few days, but 8th grade guys are pretty resilient. By the end of the week, I heard several guys, right before lights off, asking `anyone with bad gas to please come to our room so we can win smelliest room.'

In most situations, it would be bad taste. In this situation, in the unique world that 8th graders live in, it was a sign of healing.

Your pal,

Steve

I'm More Afraid Of The Chocolate Milk
— *February 18, 2003*

Urban legend on the RVA campus is that whenever the milk goes south, they announce a special treat and give the children chocolate milk to mask the south-ness. I don't know if it is true, but it is as prevalent as the man with the hook in these parts.

Because of the attack on a boarding school similar to RVA in Pakistan, we are considered a `soft' target and have begun lots of drills in case of attack. We are in a rural area of Kenya, so it is unlikely that anything will happen, but with 500 children here, we need to be extra precautious.

We had a drill like week, and went into a lockdown. A lockdown means when the alarm rings, go to the closest building, and get down and quiet. This was done in Pakistan, and no children were killed.

The kids took it seriously, and everyone cooperated, but later I did hear this line in the cafeteria:

Him1: Were you afraid during the lockdown?
Him2: I was more afraid of the chocolate milk.

I try to go into the valley once a week to visit a different school in the feeding program and make sure all is going well. The pastor who I usually go with had his cell phone stolen, and so it was hard to make connections with him. When I go, I drive on the most horrible non-roads you can imagine, and nothing has happened.

Yesterday, I was helping someone deliver some furniture, and not 30 steps from my house, there was a large truck in the middle of the road. A Kenyan man waved me through.

That was my first mistake.

While owing to no known prejudice except this: All Kenyans always believe you can get through on any road. I'm sure most of it is due to the fact that most Kenyans don't drive, so they don't know how to estimate the way a driver would.

Anyway, the glamorous missionary went into a ditch 30 steps from his home and had to get jacked out. While I was there, everyone I had ever known drove by and their expressions were all identical: you poor stupid guy.

I felt pretty stupid, and while doing no damage except cosmetic to the car, I was pretty bummed by it all. It was one of those `why am I here?' moments that happen every few months or so.

But the next morning, I went for a run. We live in a very hilly area, and I'm from two flat places: Illinois and Texas. Before I came to Africa, I had never run hills.

There is this one course we always run, and I have never been able to run the entire hill. This morning, for the first time, I ran the entire course; I made it to the top. It was such a great feeling.

I would like to say that I learned a high spiritual principle, but the only principle I can think of is that it would be better for me to walk than drive.

Every year, the junior class holds a banquet for the seniors. It is a huge event, with all the junior parents coming in to help build the set, make the food, and light the luminaries that set the pathway while the seniors walk up in their finest clothes and the entire student body cheers them on. It's a wonderful affair, and the work involved is enormous.

It occurred to me that as much emphasis as we put on the big things in life, it is the things that don't get the attention that usually have the lasting value. There is a senior here who is the captain of the soccer team, president of his class, and has a 4.0. These are all great accomplishments. He is a genuinely nice kid, and his humbleness and great sense of humor make him liked by all. There are many young ladies interested in him.

But the girl he asked to the banquet has never been asked out before in her life. She is a pretty girl, although she is so insecure that she doesn't believe it, and that insecurity tends to manifest itself in ways that aren't always pleasant. But he really thought that she was the one he should ask to the banquet.

I wish you could have seen her face as they walked up past the crowds. They just went as friends, and they both knew it, but she was glowing; it is the only way you could describe her. I looked at some friend's faces as they looked at her, and I suspect their face mirrored mine; it was hard not getting misty knowing what his gesture had meant to her.

We look at the grades, and the sports, and the size of our houses, but there are other things that really define us. This young man has accomplished many things, and he has a legitimate chance at getting into Harvard. I think he is destined for greatness. But I know, as the years go by, the only thing I will really remember when I think of him is her face.

Your pal,

Steve

PS. We are close to having Internet here. If you use AOL/ IM, could you send me your screen name? I want to test the system. Please also consider this an advanced warning that our email address will be changing soon.

Your Pal, Steve

In Their Eyes and Feet
— *March 2, 2003*

Nancy went to the woman's retreat this weekend, and so it was the older boys and I managing the care of the Dynamic Duo. It is so interesting how twins look at life differently. When we read Lyle the Crocodile, Ben points out every red car in the story. Katie shows me all the shoes that the characters wear.

This takes on huge significance, because Katie carries shoes around with her all the time, and they end up in interesting places. Nancy is always on top of that stuff, but I tend to believe that the shoe fairies will return them to their rightful place.

This morning, it was up to the three oldest Peifer males to dress the youngest Peifer female. This shouldn't be a tough thing to do, but I am always challenged by female clothing. This morning was one of rushing around, and Matthew offered to dress Katie (after I changed her diaper, of course).

The top had a flower, so LOGICALLY the leggings, to match, also had to have a flower on it. It proved a jarring contrast, so JT's solution was to find the brightest red socks to further balance the outfit. My contribution was my inability to find two shoes that matched, so she wore her beach sandals.

We are used to stares that a mixed family can receive, but I'm not sure that I have ever received the stares we got this morning. A very nice older Kenyan woman came up to us and said `Is the momma sick?' I have enclosed a picture of our fashion statement.

We went to Kamuyu this week. It is the school without any water, and so to cook the lunches, people haul water for miles in order to cook the maize and beans. The `kitchen' is about _ of a mile from the school. The kitchen had a steel roof, but someone stole the steel, so it is just a shell of a building. We are trying to help them complete a water tank that would store rainwater; the pictures show what has been done already.

I was walking with one of the parents, and he asked me what I thought of the school. I told him I admired that they were trying, but it was hard to understand the poverty from a western perspective.

He said `People try to hide their poverty, but there are two places you cannot hide it. Look in their eyes and look at their feet.' I counted over 80 kids before I found a child wearing shoes.

The look on one child's face as he waited for food captured what he was talking about. There is a longing, and a fear that chills me every time I see it.

Children shouldn't have that look. So many of them here do.

Your pal,

Steve

PS. We are scheduled to go to court Tuesday. We are hoping that we will walk away with the adoption completed, but Kenya is a funny place; we would appreciate your prayers.

PPS The water tank, inside the tank, the kitchen, a student hoping for food, and the fashion statement.

They Pled Their Own Case
— *March 11, 2003*

The paralegal told us to show us promptly at 9 AM to court. We had heard horror stories of how long this could take, so we drove two hours to the court with food, drinks, magazines and a nervous feeling.

Our first surprise was that our paralegal had become our lawyer. It was such a long process that our paralegal graduated from law school and became our attorney. We didn't know this until that morning.

We also didn't know that she had only tried one case, and she was back in court with the other people trying to get the adoption through. Many people have to go to court multiple times to get adoptions finalized.

After a very short wait, we were ushered into the court. We sat in the back row, and the judge was in the front, with our lawyer right in front of us.

As the judge began his questions, Nancy noticed that our lawyer had a booklet entitled `Trying Adoptions' that she had highlighted and was referring to during the procedure. I doubt that it would happen in the states that way, but that was how it was going.

All six of us were in the back seats, and the babies happily walked between all of us requesting to be picked up at different times. They were having a wonderful time, saying Mama and Daddy and JT and Matt, asking to be picked up, asking to be put down, and noticing all the shoes in the room and how much noise you could make hitting a metal filing cabinet.

The judge then asked why the birth father had not signed off on the adoption. The birth mother had, and I thought: here we go; it's going to be a long process. But our attorney consulted her book, and responded.

The judge questioned further, but the social worker was from that tribe, and she was able to elaborate on specifics to his questions.

This was the point where we were really getting nervous, but the judge said he would accept it. Then he looked at the babies, who were making a fair amount of noise, and said `There are only some people that I'm fine with making a racket in my court.'

Then he said `Based on the interaction between the babies and the parents, and the babies and the older brothers, the court believes that it is in their best interests to stay with you.'

As Nancy said, the babies pled their own case.

Our reactions were worthy of note. Nancy and I started to cry, Matthew let out a big WHEW (he has had nightmares that they would be taken from us), JT picked up Katie and hugged her and she gave her million dollar smile, and Ben turned to me and said `Cracker?'

Somebody needed to stay focused on the important stuff.

To the many who prayed, to the many who have helped us with the costs involved (we are still not sure of all the costs), to the many who encouraged us through this process, we are as grateful as we can be. Thank you, and we look forward to the opportunity to introduce you to Ben and Katie someday.

Just make sure you have some crackers handy when you do.

Your pal,

Steve

The Power Of One Good Man
— *March 30, 2003*

Ever since I wrote my first philosophy of life `Always Follow a Schmuck' dozens have asked me if I would continue because the first was so helpful. Actually, no one has asked, but it seemed like a cheap and easy opening for the topic of `What I have learned being a dorm dad to eighth grade boys:'

1. We had a progressive dinner for the eighth grade class. My first philosophy of life is this: If you live in a house with 16 8th grade guys, Mexican food should NOT be on the menu.
2. We had a dorm party and had an activity with the 8th grade girl's dorm. We played a game named `Plague' which involves people getting the plague and dying by screaming loudly. My second philosophy of life is this:

Any game that encourages 8th grade girls to scream is a BAD idea.

Because of the war, the decision was made to close the school a week early, so kids could get home to their parents. Borders can close, and so the school closed.

Getting hundreds of children home in the last minute is a logistical nightmare, and it proved to be so. Some of the parents don't have phones; they might have a neighbor that has one who is a hundred miles away. Getting it all taken care of took lots out of everyone.

One of the consequences of the war was the regular interim had been cancelled. Interim is a week of junior and seniors going on special trips to study marine biology or geology or aviation. It might include rafting the Nile, or climbing Mt. Kilimanjaro. It is a big part of the tradition here, and it was really a hard decision to cancel. In the interest of safety, it was determined that it would be best to reschedule with events closer to campus.

The person I would like to be like more than anyone in the world is my boss, Mark Buhler. He would never believe it, because I spend much of the day making Canadian jokes to him. (Example: To score BIG points with Canadians, play Born in the USA as loud as you can while you accept any apology with a `Oh it's ok; you're Canadian!') He is all that you would want to be: wise, compassionate, funny and someone who has accomplished so much. He is in the process of building an orphanage; he has done more to protect the forest than anyone I know, and you could go on and on and on and not cover all he has done.

When the regular interim was cancelled, it fell upon Mark to reschedule things closer to campus. Scheduling things in Africa is so hard; many businesses don't have phones, and trying to coordinate activities for 150 kids would be the most daunting task. I would estimate that Mark spent over 70 hours a week for two weeks coming up with alternatives. This was above doing his regular duties.

And then school was cancelled and all the kids went home.

I think I am learning that it is not only doing good things, but the spirit in which we approach them that is the key to greatness. If I had worked so long and hard on something that came all to naught, I would have put on my cranky pants and slept in them.

But Mark smiled his smile and just went on.

Mark is a reminder to me of the power of one good man. From the orphanage to the forest, he is accomplishing great things.

But I think the most beautiful thing he's ever accomplished was the thing that never came to be.

Your pal,

Steve

Congratulations! You Are Officially Declared An Epidemic!
— *September 20, 2003*

With four sons, I have never found them with the slightest interest in what they wore. And they were easy to dress. Woman's clothing is different. Sometimes you button it from the front; sometimes from the back. There are NEVER instructions.

It's worth it all when I finally get Katie's dress on correctly. She wears one on Sunday, and as we walk to church, there is no other word to describe it. She STRUTS. She looks good, and she knows it.

It's FUN to have a daughter. And to be fair, whenever I tell Katie her hair looks nice, Ben puts his hand on his head, and I say `Your hair looks really good too.'

We have a new group of dorm guys this year, after three years with the other group. As hard as it was to say goodbye, having new guys has reminded me of the sacrifice that their parents make.

One of the guys is a foot shorter than the other 17 other guys in the dorm. He is an eighth grader, like all the other guys, and it is first time away from his parents. The first week he struggled so hard to keep it together. We went for a walk one day, and he told me that his Dad is a pilot who flew sick people to hospitals in remote areas. His dad is the only pilot in an area that has hundreds of thousands of people in it. If his dad were to leave, people would not be able to get emergency help. And there are no schools around there…

He started crying. He felt like his dad was doing the right thing, but it was so hard to be away. I'm so inadequate in this job, and the only thing I could think to say got lost in my own tears.

The great thing about 8th grade guys is a week later, this guy is running and playing and doing well. When you are where you are supposed to be, things work out.

Which should have NO bearing on the following information: we are officially in an epidemic!!

We have discovered that if 90 or more people catch the same virus and suffer the same symptoms, it is considered an epidemic. It is something to be an epidemic in a large place, but when 100 people get it all around you, you look at it a different way. In our dorm, 14 of our 18 guys came down with high fevers and horrible persistent coughs. Matthew got it, Ben and Katie got it, and I got it.

It spread SO swiftly, and so many people were so sick, that the head of disease control in Kenya came to campus to make sure it wasn't SARS. (It wasn't) He was rather gleeful because he could trace the virus from the person who brought it to campus, and the progression to every dorm.

We are recovering slowly, but the babies got it bad, and they haven't slept through the night for almost a week, so we are hopeful for a full nights sleep soon.

We are restricted from being in the community until this passes, because I can't imagine how tough it would be to go through this without medicine. But I can report to you that because of your kindness, we were able to deliver over 100 tons of food to 20 schools. We delivered much of the maize when school was in session, and children were cheering when the truck drove up. You've fed 6500+ children for three months.

I went down to Kijabetown to see how it was going, and some of the maize wasn't dried, so they were going to dry it for a few days. I wasn't feeling good and delivery NEVER goes right and there were more glitches than usual and than I noticed him:

His soccer ball is a bunch of plastic bags you might get from the grocery store tied together with some twine.

It may have been a rough couple of weeks, but I've got it so easy. It's a shame I keep having to be reminded.

Your pal,

Steve

It Is A Two-Stroke Penalty If You Hit The Warthog
— *April 7, 2003*

We are having an identify crisis of sorts in our home. Every Peifer male has gone through being called Bubba. It's a Texas thing, and Ben really is a Bubba; just a big old sweet guy. Although most of us call him Bubba from time to time, that is how Katie always refers to him.

The problem is this: that is how Ben refers to KATIE. He calls her Bubba all the time. I've told him that if this continues, we would have to move from Texas to Arkansas.

I hated to threaten him like that, but there ARE limits, you know.

We had another one as a family. We are missionaries, so the presupposition might be that we ENJOY going to church. But we have not been able to sit through an entire service of the African church we attend when school is not in session.

African church services are long, and guests will unexpectedly show up to sing. Last week, one of the groups showed up and performed a song for a long period of time that sounded like the piano and the chorus were having a fight. They both sounded nice separately, but together, it was a LONG battle. In addition, there is no nursery, so the one-year-old dynamic duo have to sit for a long time.

Ben is our book boy, and he is fine reading, until he sees something that excites him in a book, and then he begins to yell whatever that word might be several times: `Horsie! Horsie! Horsie! Horsie! Each time he is a little louder.

Katie, on the other hand, becomes rather distressed with life in general. There is no good way to sit, or any good books to read, or anything good about anything at a certain time in the service. She does the logical thing, which is to cry like she has both hands placed on broken glass.

We can handle most of that. This week, in response to the cries, our faithful dog came running into the service to rescue the babies from whatever was troubling them. Nancy, who is as good at keeping a straight face as anyone I've ever met, lost it pretty completely and we were forced to leave early again.

Before the twins are in college, I'm sure we will sit though another service again.

We had an opportunity to take two days away and go to a game park. The Ark concept is a little like Jurassic Park. You are escorted into this building in the middle of a wild area, and then locked in for the night. The have lights all around, and natural salt licks, so you can watch as the nocturnal animals come to do what animals do at night. We saw rhino, bushbucks, elephants and a host of animals. They had an alarm system, and your room would get buzzed, as different animals would come.

The next day we went to a hotel nearby for the day. Part of the package was golf and horseback riding. The older boys and I went golfing in the afternoon, and on one hole there were three warthogs, a dozen or so baboons, and several Thompson Gazelles. I wasn't worried about baboons or gazelles, but warthogs have a reputation for being pretty ferocious, so I wondered how they would react to being struck by a golf ball. This was the actual conversation:

Me: What happens if you hit a warthog?

Caddie: It is a two-stroke penalty.

After golfing, we went for a horseback ride. I've mentioned several surreal moments in Africa, but holding Ben on a horse while we went down a trail and as we turned a corner went face to face with four giraffe was about as out there as it gets. The wisdom of bringing one year olds on horses occurred to us afterwards, but it was something none of us will ever forget.

The rooms were very tiny in the Ark, and Katie got fussy around midnight, so I took her downstairs to look at the animals. It was midnight, and no one was awake. As soon as we sat down, a large elephant came and stood directly in front of us for almost fifteen minutes. Katie kept telling me all about the elephant (Big ears, Big nose) and it was such a special moment.

I'm sitting in the dark, holding my baby girl, and the thought goes through me: I so did not want to get out of bed, and I'm having one of the neatest experiences of my life. How many times has He tried to bless me, and I believed it to be a curse instead?

This has gone long, but it has been an extraordinary week. We have been able to expand the school feeding program from five schools to twelve schools. We will be able to feed about five thousand children a day. My rough estimate is that we will purchase almost fifty tons of maize and beans. Thank you again for what you have done.

Finally, RVA is almost one hundred years old, and has never had a student accepted into the Ivy League. Not one.

Until today.

The young man I wrote about several weeks ago, the one who took the unpopular girl to the banquet, was accepted at Harvard.

Several months ago, when I started the position as the college counselor, one of the students said to me that RVA students weren't good enough to get into the Ivy League. That haunted me, and I so wanted our students to know that RVA kids would compete with anyone.

Opening that envelope was one of the most fulfilling moments in my life. I know I must sound like a complete wuss, but I just held that envelope and cried and cried and cried.

In Africa, you don't usually get to see the good guys win one like this.

Your pal,

Steve

In Africa, Do NOT Touch The White Man's Radio
— *April 25, 2003*

Last week, I was pretty impassioned about one of the RVA kids getting into Harvard, and loudly proclaiming that he was the first kid at RVA to get into the Ivy League. I checked this with the former superintendent, the present superintendent, the guidance director and the principal.

However, I did not check this with the coolest person on the planet, the person who did this job before me. She informs me that lo, not even two years ago, a student was accepted into Brown, another Ivy League school. In fact, there were probably THOUSANDS of kids accepted into the Ivy League.

What have I learned from this? Secretaries know everything; always go to the source. He is the first into Harvard, but not into the Ivies, so please forgive my error. Another student was accepted into Stanford, but no claims on the first ness of it all.

People ask if we ever get homesick, and I tell them not often. We're so busy that it's hard to find time to BE homesick. But something happened this week that made me VERY homesick.

Stacy is getting married this summer, and I won't get to see her wedding.

I've known Stacy since she was a baby. Always a nice kid, she became something more a few years ago. We became nursery partners at church. For five years, we worked together in the nursery once a month.

We were an ideal pair. I would lie on the floor and eat pretzels, and Stacy would do all the work. Because she was such a cute kid, lots of young boys would come back to visit her, and I would enlist them to do more work, so I could get on with my laying and pretzel eating.

I've missed James wedding, and Megan's wedding, and I'm probably going to miss David's wedding. I even hate going to weddings, but those kids were special to me and it was so hard to miss that special day.

So, this is an open invitation. Since I can't go to Stacy's wedding,

Everyone who reads this is probably invited in my place. If you can sing Neil Diamond songs for her on her special day, so much the better.

Just tell her that one really sad guy in Africa sent you.

We delivered more food for the school lunch program this weekend. All in all, it will be almost 70 tons of food. We are so grateful for what you have enabled us to do.

Coordinating twelve schools without phones is a nightmare. The bean truck didn't show up for five days, and we found that we had so much maize that we had to deliver it in shifts; the trucks just couldn't support that much weight. Because the headmasters were waiting for us and we were running late, one of the pastors and I started driving to schools to let them know we were behind.

Pastor Jeffery is a young man, and so he felt obligated to turn my radio up loud enough to scare away dangerous wild animals. I am an old man, so I turned it down lower, so it wouldn't damage the nearby plants. This went on several times, until I got to say a line I realized I had ALWAYS wanted to say:

In Africa, do not touch the white man's radio.

Pastor Jeffery didn't understand why I was laughing so much, but I sure cracked myself up.

I had a weird goal this time out.

My goal was to lift the bags like my Kenyan friends do. In the past, when I lifted the 200-pound bags, I had to do it with someone.

I didn't even tell Nancy, but for three months, I lifted weights every M-W-F at 6 AM trying to increase my strength so I could do it like the other guys. I just didn't want to be the old white guy who took pictures; I wanted to be more of a part of it.

When the first bag was put on my back, I tottered over to the door like I had been drinking, but I got the bag put down without a problem.

So I did it again. And again. And was able to lift ten bags.

I wish I could explain why it was such a thrill. I don't understand why it was such a thrill.

But it was.

The biggest thrill of all is that the cost of feeding a child a lunch 6 days a week is a little over a dollar a month. When we counted transportation, the cost of the maize, beans and oil, our helpers that helped us lift the 70 tons, the cost is $1.06 per student per month.

What a great thing you all are doing.

Your pal,

Steve

Your Pal, Steve

Teaching Formal Dining Etiquette to 8th Grade Guys: Mission Impossible
— *May 24, 2003*

It's been a month since my last email to you all. To my college roommate who inquired, I will tell him that the combination of changing software and computer systems took much longer than expected, with more bugs than a reasonable person might expect. To the rest of you who enjoyed the break, it's over. Anyone who is interested in how I handled it might get an idea from watching the Hulk in theaters next month.

I knew there would be lots of changes with a daughter, but one of my favorites is hair. We don't comb Katie's hair exactly; we use a pick, and then we braid it.

After her hair is picked, it is often MY turn to have my hair picked. For those that don't know me, there isn't much left to pick, and the rest is so straight that a pick is probably not the greatest tool to use. This hasn't deferred Katie, and so don't be surprised if the next time you see me there isn't a bit of curl in my hair.

We had the eighth grade formal recently. It is a tradition at RVA; the sponsors of the class put together a big dinner and they try to make it as fancy as they can. They sent us a *20 page* document to review with our guys on formal manners.

I truly love these guys, but it was as close to mission impossible as anything we have done out here. We asked my former students from last year for tips about the formal, and to a student, each guy had one comment:

Make sure the food is good.

This did not bode well for a formal evening, but we pressed on. Nancy set out a formal table, and tried to explain what each utensil was for. That was interesting in itself, but when we tried to explain some of the rules of fine dining, it really got fascinating:

Nancy: Never leave the table unless you are ill.

Them: *(Actual Question)* If you have stinky gas but it isn't loud, do you have to leave?

Me: Make sure you cut your meat in small pieces.

Them: *(Actual Question)* If you are cutting your meat and it slides off and hits a girl in the face, can you get another piece of meat?

Nancy: Put your napkin on your lap.

Them: *(Actual Question)* If you spill something on a girl, are you supposed to wipe her off?

The big day came, and I got to tie ties for at least 10 of the guys, and fix the rest of them. It was raining (more on that later) and so I drove the guys down to the cafeteria, which is where the gala event was to occur. When one of the guys saw a few of the girls (who all looked very lovely) he shouted `We are SO dead' and no one laughed. That's how they felt, but when they came home, they all commented on how much they enjoyed it. Being a dorm parent can be trying, but getting to see a bunch of guys enjoy a rite of passage is very rewarding.

It has rained here for the last month almost every day, which has made it so difficult for people who live in mud homes, which is most of the people who live around here. We've had more rain than anyone can remember, and while it is great to see everything green, so many people are cold, and so many homes are falling apart.

Kijabe is in a high elevation. Because of that, it is colder than most places in Africa. I don't know anyone who has a heating system in Africa; when it is cold, you put on more layers. Yet for many Africans, one set of clothes is all they have. Imagine being cold and never being able to get warm. We don't have heat in our home, but it is stone and we are dry.

It came home when I visited a new school we are feeding this week. Because of the rain and a concern about terrorist activity (BA cancelled all flights to Nairobi) we have needed to stay close to campus. The roads are so bad that two of the schools still don't have their food; we can't get close enough to deliver them without getting stuck.

I got to speak to a classroom, and I told them the food was from people in the United States who loved Jesus and loved them. I told them that it was important that they did well, because they were the future leaders of Africa and a great nation needed great leaders. I said `Africa is a great nation.'

Tepidly, a few students said yes. So I said it louder: Africa is a GREAT nation!!' This time, several shouted `YES!!'

So I said it at the top of my lungs: `Africa is a GREAT NATION!!!'

The yell of yes went on for over thirty seconds. Sometimes, it is good to be me.

This school has 850 students and 14 staff members. The pictures show the long lines of children waiting to get fed. While kids were waiting for their food,

I was talking to them about this and that. One little girl came up and said `Thank you for your food.'

I asked her when she ate. She told me that she ate at lunch Monday through Saturday, and her parents prepared a meal at home on Sundays.

I asked her if it was good food. She told me it was very good, but her favorite part of it was that it made her feel warm. I wasn't sure I understood, so I asked her what she meant. She told me that during the rainy season, she was always cold, but eating hot food made her feel warmer.

Sometimes I just need to look away.

Your pal,

Steve

Your Pal, Steve

You Are Not Young; Celebrating Birthdays In Kenya
— *May 29, 2003*

Nancy and I had the opportunity to visit Empuet Nursery School, which is to our knowledge the only pre-school serving the Masai tribe. This is significant because the Masai are herdsmen, and do not believe in educating their children.

They do believe in free food, and because of this, many of their children are allowed to attend this school. It is special to us, because the church it is held in was built by one of our heroes, Jim Hoeksema, and four years later it is still serving the community.

There is no good way to get to the school. It is in the middle of nowhere, and there are no good roads to it. After some of the roughest ride we've had, we arrived at the school.

Masai children have an interesting way of greeting an adult. They walk up to you and extend the top of their heads to you; your response is to place your hand on their head. It is endearing and sweet, unless they have been amusing themselves by throwing cow manure at each other. Several of the heads seemed to be fairly well coated, but we just grinned and greeted.

It's easy to look at where the children live, and what they wear, and how little they eat, and tend to despair, but as we left, I felt like I was at the beginning of a revolution. Ultimately, education is such a key to lifting this country to a different place. Tradition is a hard beast to kill, but as a saw those eager faces, I had a hope I hadn't had before.

As we drove, I told Pastor Jeffery that Nancy's birthday was tomorrow. It is a standing joke among all the pastors that I am very old. I explained to him that although I was very old, my wife was very young. He looked at her and said `You are not young.' In fact, he repeated it several times, which got funnier every time. Finally, because we were laughing so much, he explained in Africa that when you call someone young, you are calling them immature, so he was trying to compliment her. Remember that the next time someone calls you old.

We have, as all families have, some odd traditions in celebrating birthdays. Perhaps the oddest started several years ago. Although Nancy is two years younger than me, there is a two week period where she is only a year behind me. We composed a song to her that goes like this:

> Only One
> Twas not two
> Only ONE
> It's so true
> Only ONE ONE ONEEEEEEEE

The song is best sung earnestly and very out of tune, which is a challenge on a song without much of a tune, but we have managed quite well. But a new dimension has been added with the dynamic duo joining in. Katie learned the song when the second time she had heard it, and often joins in.

But Ben doesn't join in. He takes control of the song. The only words he knows are `One' but when it comes to that part of the song, he sings as if his very life depended on maximizing the volume.

I think every birthday should be celebrated at full volume.

And I hope you will join me in celebrating someone who is the most special, especially because she is so young.

Your pal,

Steve

Teenager Revolutionizes Diaper Changing Technology
— *June 8, 2003*

Nancy and I had a meeting to go to, and the older boys volunteered to watch the babies. It is truly heartwarming to see them together, except when the deed is done, and then there is great wailing and gnashing of teeth. Apparently, while we were gone, there was a major deed done.

We met the boys and the babies at the cafeteria. After we had eaten, JT invited us to 'sniff Ben's neck.' When we did, he informed us that after the deed, Ben still did not smell acceptable, so he did what any teenager would do: he covered Ben's neck with cologne.

I never understood the phrase 'he smiled weakly' until I had a teenager.

I had the opportunity to visit Longonot Primary School this week. It is a school that appears to be in the worst condition of all the schools we support.

As the children lined up for their food, it appeared that their clothing was in the worst condition of all the children I had seen.

The children were generally as happy as most schools we visited, but it was hard to not be affected by how poor they are. I start to fall between two valleys: getting depressed or getting hardened in my heart. There is another place to go, but it's not easy for me to get there. Lately, as I've left a school, the old civil rights song 'We shall overcome' has been the one I've been singing. Do you remember how it goes?

> *We shall overcome*
> *We shall overcome*
> *We shall overcome one day*
> *I know*
> *Deep in my heart*
> *I do believe*
> *We shall overcome one day.*

As I left Longonot, students from another nearby school started running over, asking me if we would add their school. We all say no to requests all the time; it's a part of life. But telling poor children that you can't add them right now is as depressing as anything I know of. I was angry, and as I was leaving, I recalled the second verse:

> We shall live in peace
> We shall live in peace
> We shall live in peace one day
> I know
> Deep in my heart
> I do believe
> We shall live in peace one day.

That didn't seem to fit, so I changed it

> We will not make peace
> We will not make peace
> We will not make peace today
> I know
> Deep in my heart
> I do believe
> We shall overcome one day.

I didn't want to give up and make peace with what is here, and I didn't want to grow depressed. I asked God to help me to have hope, because this is a place where you feel like you are always putting Band-Aids on gaping wounds.

I found hope yesterday. We went to New Life Orphanage for their annual open house. We brought the babies and Matthew, and it was a fun day of games and seeing abandoned babies who are now flourishing.

The hope part of the day was this: when we began the process of adopting, almost 60% of the babies were adopted by white families. Today, almost 80% of the adoptions are Kenyans adopting Kenyans.

As I sat watching Kenyan families walking and playing with their babies, with Ben in my lap, it was just such a sign of hope. Kenyans saving Kenyans.

Deep in my heart, I do believe.

Your pal,

Steve

The Glory and the Folly
— *June 18, 2003*

The students left for school on Friday at noon. They weren't due back until Monday afternoon, so it meant a long weekend. In the states, we could go camping in Tyler, or go to Six Flags, or hit the pool.

In Africa, you can drive just a few hours, and go to the largest game park in Kenya. We left about 7:15am on Saturday and arrived around 1:30pm. It was about 120 miles away. Even with a thirty minute rest stop, why would it take so long?

The answer is that the road to Masai Mara is one of the worst in Africa. You spend five hours jarring your body and ruining your car to arrive at ten thousand miles of unspoiled undeveloped country. It is so spectacular that any words do it an intense disservice.

They have several different camps within the park, but the signage is so limited that we were grateful we were going with friends who had been there before. We were staying in a tented camp, but one look at the dynamic duo and they decided, for reasons unknown, to put us in a cabin.

We went out after lunch for our first drive, and we saw a herd of Thompson & Grants gazelles, and about a hundred of them began running. They can leap distances of 20-30 feet. As they ran in front of us, we felt like we were in the middle of National Geographic.

Just a little later, we saw some giraffes that had arranged themselves in ways we hadn't seen before.

We were all in the same room, and this was a thrill for the babies. They were so excited that they managed to change beds every few minutes. I had the following discussion with Katie:

Katie: Daddy up?

Me: Momma's sleepers, J.T.'s sleepers, Matthew's sleepers, Bubba's sleepers, and Daddy's sleeper's. Time for Katie to go sleepers.

Katie: (Two minutes later) Daddy up?

This went on and on into the night. It was a long one.

The next morning, we saw three cheetahs walk right in front of our car. It is a wild place, and we have never seen a patrol car. In Kijabe, the police don't have money for gas in their vehicle. I don't know if it is the case at the park, but if your car broke down, you wouldn't expect help right away. And if you got out, you would be eaten.

That second night, the babies were tired and slept well. The problem was the mosquitoes, and they made the night miserable. As I head out in a month to my 30th high school reunion, the prospect of looking like I was broken out with pimples cheered me immensely; perhaps they will cover the wrinkles.

On our last morning, we were doing some serious off-roading, and went near a small bush near grass the height of our car. When we looked carefully, we saw a large lion that moved when Katie yelled. His head was bigger than her whole body.

As we were leaving the park, we saw a leopard in a tree with a fresh kill; the victim was dripping. As we watched, it jumped out of the tree in front of our car and walked into the bush with its food.

There is nowhere in America you could experience nature like this. It is the most magnificent place you can imagine.

The puzzlement was when we left, and drove the horrible roads back to Kijabe. This is the biggest tourist attraction in Kenya, and you can't easily drive there. The roads are so atrocious. Why would you allow this happen to a national treasure?

There is so much about this place that makes no sense to me at all. I wonder about it, and I wonder how much I am like Africa: What are the treasures in my life that I don't recognize and don't protect?

Your pal,

Steve

Fasting and Lean-To's: Twins Turn Two
— *July 7, 2003*

We celebrated the twins 2nd birthday on July 6th. Last year we celebrated it on July 7th. It isn't another quaint Kenyan tradition. The reason is pure Kenya.

The original documentation we had on the babies indicated they were born on July 7th. When we got closer to the adoption, we got information that one (we weren't sure which one) was born on July 6th and one was born on July 7th. When the adoption was final, we were told that they were both born on July 6th. When we got the final paperwork, it said that one baby was born on July 7th and the other was born on March 7th. While still deplorable, if that were the case, you might understand the abandonment a bit more.

Our final final paperwork says July 6th. That's our story, and we're sticking with it.

The babies are at a fun stage of life. Katie delights in running down the hall and yelling `Daddy, I *fasting.'* Ben enjoys Katie for the most part, but when he wants to get on her nerves, he puts his head on her shoulder and *leans* on her. This causes her no end of grief, but it is hard to discipline when you are trying not to laugh.

School ends on Thursday, and we say goodbye to our dorm guys. They will move on to dorm parents who are young and cool, and mostly, ones that can stay up later than 9:30 pm. It is hard to say goodbye; harder than I expected. We've had some of these guys for three years and most of the rest for two years.

In August of 2001, we had our first dorm meeting. Six different guys struggled with gas that night, and I remember thinking `it's going to be a LONG two years.'

But as with so much of life, the road that we are given can be full of blessings, even if you are blind to its values at the beginning. I have been so blessed by being the dorm dad for these young men, and I would not have bet that I would have said that two years ago. We gave them giraffe necklaces (we are Twiga dorm, which means giraffe) and awarded them a bottle of Johnson's baby powder. The reason?

When you are in ninth grade at RVA, you can go to video night and hold hands. Baby powder can reduce embarrassing sweaty palms.

I went to Nyakinyua School this week. It is a school more remote than most, and it was a tough drive to get there. There are 350 students, and three teachers. Against almost impossible odds, there does seem to be education going on there.

The headmaster told me that about 40 children are AIDS orphans. They live with grandparents, and that explained why so many of the children received their food and started running: they were going home to share it with their families.

As I was leaving, I saw a child, and I experienced that hit in the stomach feeling. Sometimes it is a look, sometimes a shape, maybe a smile, but one of the children will remind me of Ben or Kate.

It's that point when this goes beyond trying to help needy kids.

I think about Ben and Katie and what their lives would be like.

It gets so personal.

Your pal,

Steve

PS. I am going to get to be all over the US in my three weeks back. I arrive in Chicago on July 15th and I will be all over the place. If you are nearby and can stop by and say hi, that would be so great.

July 20th: Speaking at: Immanuel Presbyterian Church 29W260 Batavia Road, Warrenville, IL 60555 (630) 393-4400

July 21st: Show up at Milwaukee Joe's in Bedford at 7:30 and eat the greatest ice cream in the world! 201 Harwood Rd (Harwood & Norwood)

July 23rd: Attention all 6am Bally's gym rats. Go to the Bally's on Preston and feel GOOD about yourself when you see how FAT and BALD I have become in a mere two years.

July 24th: Shelbyville, Kentucky

July 24-25th: Kentucky Vineyard Christian Fellowship 1413 East Broadway, Campbellsville, KY 42617

July 27th: 9:45. First Presbyterian Church of Grapevine is at 1002 Park Blvd

      10:45: Colleyville Christian Fellowship in Colleyville – 3508 Glade Road, Colleyville

      2:00 Refuge Fellowship Carroll Baptist Church, 1280 E. Highland in Southlake

      6:30 Private residence. Please RSVP

July 28th and 29th North Carolina

July 30th Cedar Rapids Iowa

July 31st Private Residence. Please RSVP

Aug 1st San Francisco

Aug 3rd Bear Creek Bible Church 137 E. Hill Street Keller, Texas 76248, Phone: 817-431-852 9:45 am

Aug 4th: Back home to Nancy and kids!!!

A Chance for Change Part II: A Way Out
— *July 13, 2003*

> *Some of you might remember a year ago when I so joyfully sent Nancy to the states for three weeks, confident that it would be a happy occasion to look after the twins by myself. For reasons I don't quite understand, she does not remember it that way. Please remember her as I leave for three weeks in the United States tomorrow.*

Anyone who has been in Africa for a while has that moment. You hit the steering wheel and just yell `Why? Why does it have to BE this way?'

Most of those moments occur when I'm at a school. I know how much of a struggle it is for parents to afford to send their children to get an education. The issue is: what do they get for their money?

The sad answer is that they don't get much. It isn't that the teachers, for the most part, aren't sincere and hardworking. But without resources like books and additional teachers (average class size is almost 60) it is unrealistic to have high expectations. Many of the teachers are not well educated; some are parents who long for more for their children but never were educated themselves.

I was talking to a teacher who scraped up the money to take a computer class at a college. After taking a class for the whole term, she still had not even SEEN a computer. She `*learned*' to type on a piece of cardboard.

Oracle, the second largest software company in the world, was, at one time, almost 40% Indian. What is interesting about that is that in ONE generation, India went from having exclusively rich and poor to the largest growing middle class in the world.

Technology changed that country.

And so what I want to try is rather outlandish considering the poor US economy and the infrastructure here.

I want to build a computer center at each school that we feed.

Instead of constructing a building, we want to convert old metal shipping containers into classrooms. The cost is so much cheaper, and the buildings will be secure. Since only one of the schools has power, we will install solar panels on the roof. With a battery, inverter and a few items, we can get set up:

Container:	$1200.00
Remodel:	$3000.00
Solar Panels:	$3000.00
Batteries:	$1000.00
Inverter:	$650.00
Charge Controller:	$350.00
Cables:	$160.00
Back up Generator	$700.00
Transport	$400.00
Construction fee:	$530.00
	$10990.00

The problem with buying computers in this country is that they don't tend to synch the chips well, so we would probably buy refurbished Dell's. I can get Pentium 3's for about $200.00 each. We would begin with ten to twelve computers @ each school.

Our software would begin with all Microsoft products: the Office Suite, Typing Tutor, Encarta and Magic School Bus. I'm hoping to be able to talk with someone from MS when I'm in the states to get a better idea of cost.

I've trained two Kenyans on the packages because I think it is important that it isn't "big whitey" coming to the rescue. A wise friend of mine told me once that the solution needs to come from the people you are trying to help. I just want to help provide the tools.

Let me add a few thoughts:

1. Don't worry about this if it is not a fit. The economy is bad in the states. It's not a problem if this isn't for you.

2. If you are supporting the school lunch program, please don't drop that to do this. They are separate programs, and both are important.

3. If this seems like a fit, you can send a check made out to AIM at the address listed below. Just include a note saying it is for the A Way Out: Computer Center Peifer - project #000336; they will send you a tax deductible receipt.

4. We will start with one school, and try to work out the bugs. If funds come in, we will keep going.

I'm so grateful for the support you have given to the school lunch program, and I think it is so important to the children. It has enabled children to stay in school, and provided proper nutrition to 5000 kids six days a week. I'm excited about the computers because if it works right, it can be a means to give them a chance to escape the inconceivable poverty here.

I just want them to have a way out.

I'm so tired of it being the way it is.

It doesn't have to be this way.

Your pal,

Steve

That Will Never Happen To Me: Fast Drying Underwear In Three Weeks Of America
— *August 25, 2003*

It didn't start well. My family bet on much weight I would gain on the trip. It might have been WISE, but it wasn't SUPPORTIVE.

The transition from Africa to America is never an easy one. You are surrounded by people who have so little, and it's so easy to feel guilty.

The flight attendant asked if I wanted the steak or the shrimp, and I started weeping. He responded by saying `It's ok; you can have both.' I struggled to compose myself, but that guy is convinced I'm a loon.

I should pause here and say I ate both.

Without incriminating myself, I am a magnet for odd people on airplanes. I made it all the way over (almost 26 hours) without any unusual encounters. Surely the curse was over.

I'm waiting for my luggage in O'Hare and this old guy sees me haul a large suitcase from the luggage carousal and we have the following conversation which is ALL true:

Old Guy: That will never happen to me.

Me: What's that?

OG: Just came from three weeks in Europe and I brought was THIS. (Points to a small suitcase)

Me: That's nice.

OG: Wanna know the secret?

ME: (fear rising up) Sure.

OG: I only brought three pairs of underwear.

Me: No response

OG: I bought this new underwear and you wash it in the hotel and it dries overnight. It's amazing.

Me: I'm 48 and I've NEVER had ANYONE tell me about their UNDERWEAR in an airport before.

Wife of Old Guy: What are you two talking about?

Me: His underwear.

WOOG: Oh, it's great! It dries so fast!

In 21 days, I stayed in the same bed once. I had determined that if I would only spend one night with someone, how annoying could I be?

I was the guest from hell.

Highlights include:

- Traveling 7000 miles and not winning the person who has come the furthest to the high school reunion (Australia) and not being the oldest father (someone had a ten month old)

- Hadn't seen my aunt in decades and falling asleep **in** the lovely dinner she made for me.

- Shouting loudly in a Wal-Mart `These Snickers have ALMONDS' and frightening an old woman, possibly the one whose husband has dry underwear.

- Managing to lose my phone list with hundred of names of people I was going to call in the first five days.

- Missing a flight and missing out on a birthday party of a dear friend and missing my one opportunity to see one of my best friends in the whole world.

- Sitting next to two very nice Tupperware distributors on their way to a Tupperware convention and trying to explain why Africa might not be their next big market.

- Having spent 48 years dodging the bullet, summoning up my courage and admitting to my younger sister that I needed her help to do clothes shopping for the children. (She is a force of nature in regards to shopping)

- Seeing an old friend who I hadn't seen in 20 years and being afraid to eat her peanut butter pie because it was so wonderful 20 years later that it couldn't possibly meet the demands of my memories, and having it be so good that I asked for it for breakfast.

- Getting in late from a delayed flight and being picked up by a kind friend who asked if I wanted a sandwich and instead whining `I WANT A PIZZA WITH AMERICAN SAUSAGE'

- On the fourth day of three breakfast meetings, wondering if I had overbooked this trip a little bit.

- Speaking at the sixth place in a day and preparing to say `You've GOT to be sick of hearing me speak' and realizing that they hadn't HEARD me speak; **I** was sick of hearing me speak.

- Being capable of leaving dirty clothes in a pristine hall while yelling `I've gotta' catch a flight; can I pick this up on Monday?'

There are so many wonderful memories of this trip; friends driving for hours to say hi, seeing family, having someone give a huge check for the computer centers and for once in my stupid life being speechless, having the amount of schools we can feed almost double, staying up late and catching up.

It was also hard; hearing bad news, sad news, and the pain that life brings. Calling someone who is getting married and knowing you can't be there; friends out of work, friends going through tough times. I went by the cemetery, and was surprised by how much it still hurts.

On my last day in the states, I stopped by my bank. There were three tellers at the bank. I waited 15 minutes in line.

My teller had been the funeral director for Stephen. I hadn't recognized her, but she remembered me. She had left the funeral home years ago, and was now working at the bank. She told me how much his life had impacted her, and how she had started making changes in her life after the funeral.

I don't know why, but when you lose a child, you have this fear that no one will remember them. It was such a gift to have that right before I left. As I left, I was reminded of something I had written several years ago:

He has gone to a place where babies never die, where the only tears are tears of joy, and there are no more separations and no more goodbyes.

It was so hard to say goodbye to Nancy and the kids, and then so hard to say goodbye to friends in the states. Thank you all for a special three weeks. I'm sorry for overbooking and not calling everyone I wanted to, but I'm so grateful for the chance I had to see so many.

There is a place, and there will be a time where we won't have to say goodbye anymore.

All that being said, saying hello to my family again made it all worthwhile. JT continued his holiday growth spurt and is now an inch taller than me, Matthew is doing great and the twins are growing like weeds. And Nancy is greater than ever, if such a thing is possible.

They told the staff that we needed to be in touch with today's youth, I was able to purchase a CD for 75 cents on line called `Forever in Bluegrass: The songs of Neil Diamond performed by a bluegrass band." I think you will agree that with THAT in hand, I'm ready to take on the next group of students when school starts tomorrow...

And no, it's none of your stinking business how much weight I gained.

Your pal,

Steve

Hawaii

— October 9, 2003

The theme song from Hawaii Five O keeps running through my head. I don't know if it is coincidence or not, but my college, Northern Illinois University, is now FIVE wins and ZERO loses and is ranked 16th in the United States, beating Maryland and Alabama in the process. And if you think THIS is obnoxious, just WAIT until the Cubs beat the EVIL Marlins.

We all have changes, but few like Matthew experienced this week. He got braces and glasses. He looks cute in his glasses and he only has to wear his braces for a year, but that is a lot for a sixth grade guy to handle. I know his father, and when he got glasses and braces, he turned into a CRABBY guy. Matthew is taking it all in stride. He is such a cool kid.

I went down to Kijabetown School to help with lunch last week. There were two parents who were using the kitchen to prepare the food.

The school has about 400 children, and they spend much of the morning getting the food ready.

The children were thanking you for the food. I asked a teacher how the food had affected her students. When I ask a teacher, I usually hear something like `They are better able to concentrate.'

This teacher said `When they hold their stomachs and cry because they are hungry, I lose hope and do not teach well. It is good when they eat.'

In every small community, there are the favorites. In ours, it is the Kings. Matt and Jan are so bright and so funny and so caring that, in the words of a co-worker, everyone thinks they are their best friends.

They were five months pregnant and lost their baby yesterday. When you are in a small place, things like that hit you harder than they might when people aren't as close. There was a just such a somber spirit here today.

I was walking through campus, and a senior guy, who has always been a fairly sullen kid, stopped to talk for a moment. I asked him how he was doing, and he said `I'm just sad' and there were tears in his eyes.

I'm not sure I can explain why, but I found great comfort in those tears.

Your pal,

Steve

Underwearing: My Reluctant Love Affair With The Hygiene Impaired
— *October 23, 2003*

I only play golf twice a year, so excuse one more golf story, ok? JT, Matthew and I are driving, and JT hits the green, and gets the greatest excuse that has ever been recorded for golf. A baboon comes running, and grabs his ball. Our caddy charges the baboon, who flees with the ball. If your putt doesn't go in after THAT, don't you have a RIGHT to a gimmee?

We all desire to create something that will live forever. Many will create something of beauty that will edify and challenge all you see it.

Mine is a little different.

When I first came to Africa in 1999, I taught computer to grades 1-6. Several kids were cutting up in class one day, and we had the following discussion.

Me: Stop it, you knuckleheads.
Them: What is a knucklehead?
Me: It means you have knuckle for head.

For some reason, `you have knuckle for head' has caught on. Sometimes, `you have knuckle' also works, but it is something that I hear many times a day.

It isn't what I would have CHOSEN to live forever.

What is it like to have 18 eighth grade guys in the house you live in? Of course, we marvel at the multi-culturalness of it all: Africans, Koreans, Germans, Danish, Americans and Australians all growing and sharing the joys of their cultures.

But, this being eighth grade guys, mostly it is gross.

Examples:

Most of these guys are hygiene impaired. One day I am inspecting the cleaning (har har har) of the toilet:

Them: I cleaned it. Honest
Me: Do you call THAT clean? (pointing to something quite disgusting)

Them: I guess not.

Me: Clean it then.

Them: (Rubbing disgusting area with bare hand)

Me: NOT WITH YOUR BARE HAND!!!

Them: (Extreme puzzled look)

Later, after an altercation between two rooms, I asked each guy to write an essay explaining why they were sorry for what they did.

Them: I am very sorry for underwearing Josh at 3 AM.

Me: I am probably going to be sorry for asking, but what is underwearing?

Them: You sneak into someone's room while they are sleeping and stuff dirty underwear into their mouths.

Me: You have GOT to be kidding.

Them: (Greater extreme puzzled look)

I can't articulate why I am enjoying them as much as I do. Nancy has a theory that I see my younger self in every disgusting act, but I'm sure she is mistaken because I was a veritable angel as a young child. It probably stems from the fact that I see the opportunity to invest in young lives, and the delight that comes with doing that.

Or I'm just so glad that underwearing wasn't invented when I was a kid.

I went to Kiambogo today. It is a school of 800 children is a very remote area. It took almost an hour to get there. When we arrived, the children were running towards the car.

The headmaster told me that he has nine teachers to instruct 800 children. He said that wasn't the greatest problem he had.

He told me his goal was to have one textbook for every three children. Nancy was at a different school this weekend, and she was told the same thing. It was such a hard thing to hear.

The headmaster was so encouraged. He told me `It is getting so much better. We have food, and we have more books. Soon we may have more teachers.'

Perspective is a real gift, isn't it?

Your pal,

Steve

Your Pal, Steve

It Not Working
— *November 5, 2003*

We have been through the toilet training routine before, but I promise it is different with twins. For that matter, everything is different with twins. Nancy once mentioned something that was harder with twins, and it made me think hard about anything that was EASIER with twins. Anyway, I put Katie down on the potty seat, and after sitting a spell, she looked up at me and said `It not working.'

The whole idea of explaining the process to a two year old is exhausting, and I'm not sure the words exist, but if you have ideas on how to clarify this to Kate, I would appreciate it.

We will begin construction on the first computer center soon. It is in a very remote area, with no power nearby, so we will use solar power. Karima has 800 students in the primary school, and 100 students in the secondary school. We just added food for the older students at the secondary school, and it was my first visit there. If there were a word to describe the students, it was that they were without hope.

They are older, and they have seen all that Africa has to offer, and it has made them afraid to hope, because anytime they have hoped, Africa has thrown it back in their face. When I told them we were going to build a computer center at their school, no one believed me.

I ran over to the primary school, and the children haven't given up. The poverty is just as bad, but they are little kids, and they still believe things can get better.

But this has been a week of reminding me that the unheralded is the most important. Nancy runs the library for the first through six grades, and they recently moved buildings. It was a huge amount of work and time, and it isn't a glamorous job. You aren't going to get a lot of attention for remodeling a library.

But they worked so hard on it. And it is such an improvement on what was here before, and it will mean so much for the parents leaving their children at the school; that they will be cared for and nourished while they are away from their parents. It's a little thing that is so big.

The guy that does all the construction is a man named Jerry, one of the great people of the planet. He just works and works and works; never a complaint, always a joke, but always great care to make sure the work is done with excellence. That can be a challenge in Africa; the right tools, the right lumber, knowledgeable labor are all huge obstacles here.

But the library is beautiful. And one of the things that is so great about this place is that they asked the hero to cut the ribbon; usually that is the big shot, but really, this time, they did pick the big shot.

I've been accused of having too many coincidences for my own good, but this one is too good to not share. I went to my 30th high school reunion this summer, and on the way home, I noticed in the information they gave us that one of my classmates worked for Hope College in Michigan. I hadn't even seen Molly at the reunion; she was pretty popular and pretty busy.

But one of our Kenyan students had been accepted to Hope, and she got to go. Her parents make very very very little a year, so extra money is rare for them. She didn't have any warm clothes, and didn't know what to do.

I emailed my classmate, and she is taking Josephine shopping. Someone I haven't seen in 30 years is going to clothe this young girl. It's a little thing, I suppose, unless you don't have warm clothes. But like the library, I'm reminded that there are no little things; that if we give ourselves to what we've been called to do, it's always big.

Molly and I went to school in Illinois. She ended up in Michigan; I'm in Kenya, and one of the students ends up at Hope, and I find out that Molly is at Hope because someone sends me a ticket to go back for my 30th reunion and I find out she is there and is willing to help out a kid without a warm coat.

I mean, you just got to love these coincidences. Or the One who created them.

Your pal,

Steve

You Can't Leave Until It's Clean; A New Revelation of Eternity
— December 1, 2003

The term ends at the end of November, and the guys get to go home for a month. Provided of course, that the dorm passes inspection by an external inspector. We began with a hope that the dorm would be clean enough to call the inspector right after lunch, and then struggled with the idea that the boys would be done by the time they got to college.

Eighth grade guys (ok, all males) but eighth grade guys especially believe that the cleaning fairies will come and do the cleaning for them if they only believe, and they must express their beliefs by wandering about aimlessly and asking `Is it done yet?' in hopeful tones. We won the award on campus for being the last dorm cleared to go, but thankfully, we did pass and they are home with their parents.

If you are like me, you sometime look for reasons not to exercise. We had another virus pass through the campus the last week of school, and several dozen kids were sick, including Nancy this time. I was as tired as I could remember, and as I contemplated running in the morning, we got a warning not to run on our usual course.

Elephants.

Right outside our campus, a herd of elephants were ANGRY, and chasing anyone who got near them. We haven't had elephants before. We get lots of baboons and monkeys, but elephants were a new phenomenon, and it seemed like a worthy reason to sleep in.

We had a British family over for Thanksgiving. This was an actual conversation with their daughter the week before:

> Me: You are coming to our house for Thanksgiving!!
>
> Her: What is Thanksgiving?

As the school year in Kenya comes to an end, you all fed almost seven thousand children six days a week. Twenty schools were blessed by your kindness, and although I don't have official statistics yet, many schools reported that they had NO drop outs vs. a usual 30-40% drop out rate. The first computer lab is coming together.

When I made an announcement to the teachers about the lab, they couldn't believe it. One teacher told me he had prayed for a miracle, but he had not expected anything this great.

My favorite Christmas song is Good King Wenceslas, and my favorite part is the end: They who now shall bless the poor shall themselves find blessings. I think of you guys when I hear it, and I pray that you have been as blessed as you have blessed.

I am the most unlikely person in the world to be doing this stuff, but I heard two stories this week that made me realize that He uses people where they are. Duanne's journey to Africa began several years ago when his daughter broke her back and became a paraplegic. Going through that changed him forever.

Last month there was a terrible car accident, and a young woman became a paraplegic because of it. They called Duanne and his wife, and they were able to minister to her in a way that no one else could have. She was comforted, and accepted the eternal Hope into her heart. What they had gone through changed the young woman forever.

Nancy and I were babysitting today, and heard the story of an abandoned three pound baby. His cries were too weak for anyone to hear, and so he was going to die.

But the ants descended on him. And as they began to feast on him, his cries became loud enough that he was found and saved. The ants, which could have been a curse, saved him.

He even uses ants. He even uses me.

Your pal,

Steve

Merry Christmas From The Peifers
— *December 20, 2003*

[from JT]

This first term in 9th grade has given me many things to think about. For one thing, the workload doesn't exactly get lighter! I used this term to figure out what I need to push harder in and where I can give slack. This break has gone well, we went to Mombassa. And as I am sure you can see I caught a 40 lb. Wahoo. Matthew and I were able to scuba dive together, and were able to go spear fishing. This term has tried me in many areas, but I will stand firm. And as Chamberlain would say: "Fix bayonets and charge!"

[from Matthew]

6th grade has proven itself a challenge. It's a lot of fun, but there are many things to accomplish. It's shown me a preview of junior high school and what kind of ambitions I need next year. Mombassa was an awesome treat. I got certified in scuba diving. To pass, I had to do certain exercises under the water eighteen meters deep. I also saw the fish I've always wanted to see: a puffer fish inflate. I'm looking forward to the rest of the year.

[from Nancy]

"Grace" is the word that best sums up this year for me. I've known God's grace in crises, but this year I've desired (and hopefully progressed) in learning to abide in that same grace in the midst of the day-to-day things— receiving as grace the fact that I didn't get sick during the flu epidemic that hit campus; accepting the grace to be patient with two very curious two-year-olds; knowing His grace in letting go of my teenager when I feel like holding tighter; trusting His grace when my own strength was depleted but there were still meals to fix, clothes to wash, and homework to help with; being more aware of His grace to continue to refine me and reveal Himself to me. Truly, His grace is amazing.

[from Steve]

All the things that happened this year, but I keep going back to a little kid who told me `I like school better when I'm not hungry.'

There were so many struggles and so many victories, but that one stays with me. We move up to 25 schools in January and over 8000 children; we are so grateful for what you have done. We pray that this Christmas is a celebration of Jesus' love for you.

Merry Christmas!

Steve, Nancy, JT, Matthew, Katie and Ben Peifer

Letters from 2004 – 2005

They Got One?
— January 11, 2004

When you give twins a bath together, they NOTICE stuff. Since we are trying to do the toilet training thing, it has led to discussions about differences between a boy and girl. After almost every bath, Katie will tell me `Ben has one, and Daddy has one, and JT has one and Matthew has one but Momma doesn't have one and I don't have one.'

That was all good, but she and I were going for a walk and we passed a friend and Katie asked `They got one?' Me, not being quick, asked `Got one what?' Katie then said `Ben has one, and Daddy has one, and JT has one and Matthew has one but Momma doesn't have one and I don't have one.'

I said, `Oh THAT one.' And I clarified that we generally don't speculate about such things. And she said `Oh'. And I'm SURE that will be the end of that.

A friend recently wrote to me about a situation at work that reminded him of the scene in `It's a wonderful life' where Jimmy Stewart yells `Don't you realize that this will mean scandal and prison?'

I knew how he felt.

The last time I bought maize the guy sold me some that hadn't been dried well. That can rot, and it also violated the contract I had with him. In addition, since then the government has recently raised prices it would pay for maize, and so all prices went up.

I got many bids, and met with a family who gave a reasonable price and they had a sturdy truck. I told them that I hadn't determined how much I would need, because I hadn't gotten a firm price, but that I would work with them. I told them that I would determine how much I could buy based on the price and get back to them.

In the meantime, they bought and delivered one thousand bags of maize.

I've been scammed many times many times in Kenya, and I don't think that is what happened. They were excited that I said yes, and they wanted to move fast in case I changed my mind.

The problem was I didn't have enough money to cover that amount. The way our accounting works is that if someone makes a donation, it can take several months for the money to get here.

And I was stuck. There wasn't a way out like in America, where I could return it.

The night before Christmas I couldn't sleep. I was sweating so much that the bed was wet. I have some extra money from selling our home, but I didn't want to touch it, but I didn't seem to have many options.

Bottom line is this: it turned out I had nearly enough in the account to squeak by. We are buying fewer beans this term. Communication is tough out here, but this one really threw me for a loop.

Part of the reason it hit me hard was that I realized: I want to look good. Sometimes you find out how much you want to do good, and how much you want to look good. I found out, again, what I really am.

It was EASY to make new years resolutions this year. I want to resign from the looking good club. (Note to all old friends especially from Kansas who LONG to write hilarious responses to this: beat ya' to it.)

It has been a tough month in many ways, JT has been sick, and Nancy and Matthew both have mild cases of pneumonia. Matthew also is experiencing high fevers whenever he stays up late, and the doctors haven't been able to figure it out.

We went to the Embassy to apply for immigration papers for the twins. If they interpret the law one way, it will be a small of amount of money when we return to the states to apply for their citizenship. If they interpret it the other way, it will mean home studies and thousands of dollars. We are trying, sometimes successfully, not to be anxious about it.

So this is a good time to mention that we return to the states in July for our furlough year. The reason for a furlough is to renew yourself, which I never understood before. But I understand that it is easy to get burned out on the field, and it is best to take a year before you have to. AIM requires one every three or four years.

Part of our motivation is we don't want JT to miss his junior and senior year at RVA. Part of it is to get citizenship for the twins. Part of it is to reconnect with family and friends. Matthew and JT have not been in the United States for three years, and Ben and Katie have never been.

A big part for me is to see if we can expand our programs. We are feeding 25 schools and 8400 students a day. I long to see many more children helped with this. We will finish our first computer center in March. I would love to return after our year's furlough with the support to do many more centers. So, if your church or organization is open, I would appreciate the chance to share our vision.

Our furlough in the states will coincide with some big events in our family: JT will turn 16 and be able to get his drivers license, Matthew will become a teenager, the twins will become US citizens, Nancy and I will celebrate 20 years of marriage, and I will turn 50.

50.

I better step it up. I've got a lot I want to get done, and I'm running out of time.

Your pal,

Steve

Your Pal, Steve

More Cross-Cultural than Ostrich Fajitas
— *January 21, 2004*

Whenever I sang ANYTHING to my little sister, she would yell `I know! You're singing the Theme from Rocky!'

I was kicked out of the choir in Manhattan, Kansas because I could make a whole row go flat, and I was kicked out as the director was making his weekly plea for more male voices.

When I was briefly on the worship team in Texas, I was told that I could sing whenever the whole band was blaring. Otherwise, I should just PRETEND to sing.

This is all to say that I don't know WHY they choose ME to lead the karaoke event on Friday. Someone actually gave a missionary a karaoke machine, and they hauled it out here. I'm not sure that anyone had done it here before, but on Friday evenings, they have Variety night, and they try to plan all sorts of different things for the kids to do.

At 8pm, there was a huge group of kids in the room. I never did karaoke in the states, but I began the evening with an inspiring version of `All My Exes Live in Texas' which was a BIG hit with the bride.. After they got use to it, I'm sure they sang as badly and with as much enthusiasm as anyone in the states.

With a couple of exceptions.

I'm in the front of the room, changing discs, and I look up: Kenyans, Koreans, Brits, Canadians, and all the rest singing along to the chorus of American Pie. It was the most multi-cultural experience I've ever had, unless you count the time I ate ostrich fajitas.

The best part was three kids singing `Stand by Me'. The first kid sang the first verse in Portuguese, the second kid sang the second verse in Korean, and the third kid sang the third verse in French. Probably not what you would hear in the states, but it was so cool.

I was going down to the valley on Thursday to visit a school, and the guy I was supposed to meet didn't show up, and the school I did go to didn't have the food ready to go, and I was frustrated, and started driving back to campus. The road I took is fairly new; not paved, and very hilly and scary in the rain. About half way up, I stopped to give a ride to two older women who were making the long hard climb to the hospital.

As they got in, it started to rain really hard. I was going uphill, and it was really slippery, and they both started to make noises that sounded like they were afraid. I was scared too.

> Me: If you all know how to pray, this would be a good time to start.

> Them: GOD!!! HELP!!!

He did, and we got to the hospital, and I drove away thinking `That's why I was supposed to go down to the school today.'

It was such a great feeling.

There is a couple here who have to leave because his father is sick and they need to go home and take care of him. They have a dorm, and it is filled with sixth grade girls, so it is not an easy assignment.

And RVA is a place that no matter what you do, you can never get it done, because we are all stretched pretty thin. It's hard to fill a position like that.

Enter Ben and Jeannie. They are a pretty unique couple. They met at Harvard as undergraduates, married, and have started many companies. They have done very very well. They have four children, and they help run the business office, and are very active in reaching out to the community.

And they volunteered to take on the dorm.

It doesn't sound glamorous, and it isn't, but so many ministries couldn't function if there weren't dorm parents. Most people don't come to Africa to sit in a dorm. When you see people who have given up so much take on another job, it makes you re-look at how you do everything.

You would never know they went to Harvard and built the many companies they had. They don't talk much about themselves. Ben spends much of his day insulting me, but they are so self effacing you would never suspect their background.

Someday, someone will probably write a book about them. They will talk about their education, and the companies they created, and their great success.

But if they don't mention the dorm, they will miss the heart of the story.

Your pal,

Steve

Your Pal, Steve

Love vs. Inhaling Helium: Valentines Day for the Eighth Grade Guys
— *March 4, 2004*

Someone brought us one of those variety boxes of different types of chips from the states. They were the kind of bags that you might have put in your lunchbox when you were a kid. It was a great thrill, and it became almost like a poker game. `I trade you two Doritos for one Cheetos.' I think I could eat one of those bags in one gulp when I was a kid; we lingered over our bags and our trades for almost an hour.

Fritos can be FUN.

Each high school class works at raising money for all of their four years to go on their senior trip, and one of the ways that sophomores raise money is by selling helium balloons for Valentines Day. Helium is hard to find in Kenya; the poor guy in charge of finding it has horror stories to tell.

We noticed that there were more balloons delivered to the dorm than one would expect-- eighth grade guys just don't generally get lots of stuff on Valentines Day; if they get anything, it's from an older sister whose motives are suspect because they know how much the guy will get teased. But we were getting lots and lots delivered, and finally found out why: they were buying them for themselves so they could inhale the helium and talk funny.

Love is SUCH an eighth grade thing.

Nancy has some books from the library that were old and outdated, and instead of throwing them away, we give them to the schools we work with. I took a box of about 12 books to a school last week. The school has almost 1,000 students, with 13 teachers.

The headmaster told me something that chilled me to the bone. He thanked me for the books, because the library had now doubled in size.

It is a long steep ride home, but some days it seems steeper than others.

We did get a report from another school that they were now requiring students to come to classes in the afternoon because the food enabled them to concentrate longer. Thank you for what you have done with this program.

And, we go "live" with the computer center this month. Sometimes things that are meaningful to me might not make sense to you because of the context, and I risk that by telling you that we experienced a true miracle with the computers. They got to our mission headquarters in NY on a Monday and they were in our house in Kenya by Friday.

The people who handle sending items to Africa from our mission headquarters have a pretty impossible job, and they do a remarkable work in spite of all the problems. For perspective's sake, I have had things stay at headquarters for four months before I received them.

In addition, I had budgeted thousands of dollars for duty and customs, and it cost me less than the two fruitcakes a nice friend of ours sent to us. We are truly blessed, but continue to ask for your prayers; there is much that still needs to be worked out.

Today is a duo anniversary for us. The twins were legally adopted a year ago today. We are making progress on all the paperwork we need to get in order to return to the states in July, but it has proved to be as difficult and stressful as anything we have done in Africa. They are worth it all, but every time we think we are getting close to being done, we find out something else we need. We just discovered that we will need to get British visas because we have a ten hour layover in England on the way home.

Whenever I feel stressed by it, Katie reminds me that in America, you can call someone nice on the phone and they will bring you a pizza. I can't wait to introduce you to them.

Stephen was born six years ago today. It used to be such a hard day, but I look at the twins, and the 8000+ kids at the schools we feed, and the amazing life we live now because of his life, and I can see him in almost everything I do, and everything I see.

Your pal,

Steve

Great Moments in Bad Acting: The Eighth Grade Attacks a Play
— *March 12, 2004*

Nancy had this conversation with one of our dorm guys the night before the big play:

Nancy: Do you feel ready?

Them: I've memorized all my lines. I just haven't figured out when I say them.

And so it was, a glorious night of missed cues, mumbling, and acting so bad it made you feel good about yourself. It was like a night in the states when you can't sleep and turn on the TV and get to watch a really really bad Japanese monster movie; so bad it is good, and you are so glad it's not you up on the stage that the world somehow seems brighter. And it was like my golf game, average with glimpses of brilliance.

Nancy and I went to make another attempt at getting the travel papers for the twins. We arrived at the immigration building at 9:00am.

9:00am: We wait in line to submit our paperwork.

9:30 am: Our turn in the lines arrives. The government official looks at our paperwork and informs us that we need dependent's passes for the twins. This is a new one for us, and we are directed to another line.

9:45 am: Another government official tells us it will take months to process the paperwork. We ask if there is any way to expedite the process. She tells us to go to the fifth floor and ask them if they will help us.

10:00 am: We leave the building and walk around to another side and get on the elevator. We jump off when we realize that there is no fifth floor that it stops on. After several attempts with several elevators, we realize that we should go to the sixth floor and walk down.

10:15 am: We knock on several doors, and are finally directed to a room where an official tells us that she will do the paperwork. We should just go back downstairs and request that the paperwork be brought upstairs.

10:20 am: We walk down the stairs and wait in line to request the paperwork be brought upstairs. We wait in line.

10:45 am: We are invited to go back upstairs with the paperwork.

10:50 am: The government official tells us she will be done at 3. We explain that we have an appointment at the US Embassy at 1:30 that we cannot miss. She tells us to come back at noon.

10:50 am: We walk downstairs and wait.

11:45 am: We walk up five floors. The government official tells us we must downstairs to pay our fees. Mindful that the offices close at 12:30 for lunch, we run down five flights of stairs and wait in line.

11:55 am: We pay our fees and run up five flights of stairs. We wait outside the office.

12:10 pm: The government official informs us that she is done, and that we should go to another office to retrieve it.

12:20 pm: The new government official tells us it will not be ready until the afternoon.

There is someone at RVA that does this kind of work full time. He refers to it as human Pac-Man. After 9/11 and the recent attacks in Madrid, you understand why a government wants to be careful. But it is hard to understand this, and the waste of time and resources days like this consume. And we are not much closer to getting the paperwork we must have to leave with the twins.

We went to a school we had never visited today; Umhatru. It is the most remote school I've ever been to since I have been going to schools. The children were not used to white faces, and one little girl cried whenever I looked at her. (Note to friends especially from Kansas: no comments necessary here)

It was desperately poor. And there was a sign on the door that would just break your heart.

What we saw was so sobering:

But the longer we were there, the children warmed up to us. The food helps.

And at the end, the little girl who had cried gave me a little hug.

It looked like a small victory, but it felt like so much more.

Your pal,

Steve

Your Pal, Steve

And I Don't NEED Sun Screen
— *April 6, 2004*

Our kids are all changing. I have this conversation with Katie almost every day:

> Katie: Daddy, what color skin do you have?
>
> Me: I have white skin.
>
> Katie: What color skin do I have?
>
> Me: You have beautiful black skin.
>
> Katie: And I don't NEED sun screen!

Whenever Nancy works on Katie's hair, as soon as she is done, she races to the mirror to see what it looks like. That is funny in itself, because Katie's run might remind you of Groucho Marx's sloping walk, but she is the only child we've had who has CARED what she looks like.

In the picture, Ben is wearing a coat that JT wore, Matthew wore, and his cousin Douglas wore. It is remarkable how clothing can evoke emotion, but it really did when I put on his jacket for the first time.

Matthew is becoming a young man, and recently wrote a piece of music that was just beautiful. The sixth graders go on a special safari at the end of the year, and he is thrilled about becoming a member of the polar club, which involves jumping in an ice fed lake. Traditions are IMPORTANT here, even weird ones.

JT is now 15, and has gone on three dates. The first girl asked him to a Sadie Hawkins movie night. She is an absolutely beautiful white young lady. The second young lady who asked him out to a Sadie Hawkins luncheon is an absolutely beautiful Kenyan woman. On his third date, he asked out a beautiful Korean woman. For more excitement, he got invited to Uganda (just a day's drive) and spent a day white water rafting on the Nile River. He asked at one point if he could get out and swim, and was told it wasn't a good idea, because the crocodiles would be too appreciative.

The computer lab is operational, and that is a story in itself. I went to a guy named Walter who I met during our orientation school for coming to Africa. He is with the technical part of our mission, the part that does the building and creating.

I told him that I wanted a computer lab. Several weeks later, he came up with an idea, a design, and a budget. Because our budget was limited and because thievery is such an issue here, he took an old metal shipping container, and Ft. Knox would probably be easier to get into than this container. Solar is gold, and he figured out how to install the solar in a way that the only way you could steal it would be to break it, which sort of negates the point.

When we got the used computers, they had a ground plug, which is not compatible with any converter plugs here, and I panicked. Walter just pulled them out; he is a guy who knows what to do, and he does it.

But what you might not know about Walter is that after he delivered the Computer Center, he lived in it for three nights to do all the work that needed to be done and protect the special tools he would need to make it function. While we were doing finishing touches today, he got out a can of paint and did touch up work. I had to walk off and cry over that; he has just done it all for this project, and done it with excellence and care that inspire me when they don't put me to shame.

But it is working perfectly. We have a teacher, and for this month, she is just going to be teaching the teachers, while the children are on break. No one at this school besides the teacher has ever seen a computer in real life, so we are starting from ground zero. I was instructing the head master about using his baby finger to type the letter A, and I told him so many times that he greets me with a wave from that finger. They are excited beyond excited.

A young man came up to me last week and told me `When you told me that you would build a computer center, I did not believe you. When the computer center came, I still did not believe it.' I invited him in and let him write his name. `Now I believe' he said with a face full of tears.

This is going to get weirdly personal, so feel free to skip through the next few paragraphs. I so desperately believe in the feeding program we do, and I pray that it can continue in May. But like much we have done in Kenya, it is reactive.

I've been in Kenya for four years, and this is the first time I've felt like I have took a stab at the beast that has robbed and raped and stolen from this country. It is a small center, and it will only serve a few hundred children, but it is a start, and a real way out of the poverty that consumes this land.

Besides the super important and obvious best days of my life (Nancy saying yes, birth of the boys and adoption of the twins) there are two other days that stand out as my top days of living.

When Stephen was born, he had such a cleft lip that he couldn't drink from Nancy or a regular bottle because he couldn't create a sucking motion. It took a special bottle, and none of the nurses were able to get him to take any milk. They said that they would need to insert a feeding tube in him.

I asked if I could try, and the nurses reminded me that they were neo-natal intensive care nurses and two of the best nurses had been unsuccessful. I asked again, and they sighed the heavy sighs that only nurses can sigh.

And he took the whole bottle from me. And he would only eat from Nancy and me, like he knew he didn't have much time, so why waste it on someone else? And that still stands as the greatest day of my life.

The other day, which has nothing to do with the previous one, was over 30 years ago. It was a summer evening, and I was in the car with Tom and Charlie and Chopper and Rocky Mountain High came on, and I loved that song and I loved my friends and I knew that they loved me and I just felt so alive and so happy.

I don't know why I thought of those two events, but as I watched Walter put on the touch up paint and I cried, those thoughts came pouring into my mind. And I realized what a gift it is to do what you all have allowed us to do in Kenya, and I would have to say thank you for giving me one of the greatest days of my life.

The Passion movie hasn't reached Africa yet, but from what I've read, the impact of the movie is the realization of the sacrifice that Jesus went through to give us a second chance. When that young boy told me `Now I believe' I realized something for the first time: part of the reason we are given a second chance is to offer it to someone else.

I'm so grateful for the second chance you have given these kids. I hope you have the greatest Easter celebration ever. And don't forget the sun screen; some of us need it.

Your pal,

Steve

Your Pal, Steve

Son of `It's Not For Me, It's For My mother'
— *April 25, 2004*

Long long ago I wrote about the trauma of having to buy personal items for my mother when I was a kid, and how when I had to buy them for Nancy, it got worse. It got a LOT worse last week.

We are about an hour away from shopping, so since I was in town, it was only fair that I would buy the product that she wanted. I went into the store, and looked and looked, and finally found the product. But Nancy had asked for Super Thin, and that was NOT on the box.

So I took a DEEP breath, and asked a clerk in the store. It is always an adventure to ask for anything in a Kenyan store, because communication can be problematic. I've asked for bread and been directed to sea salt. But it is FAR worse when you have no idea what you are asking for. I have absolutely no concept of what Super Thin means, and a horror of ever finding out. But I had to ask:

> Me: Is this Super Thin?
> Her: Do you want wings?
> Me: I have no idea what that means. Please don't tell me.
> Her: It will probably be ok.

Never again.

This has been a month to ponder the eternal. The Petts, some fellow missionaries we met three years ago were murdered in Uganda. They were nice people; former dairy farmers who sold their farm to come to try to help in Africa. They were teaching at a technical school, and they were murdered and the school was burned.

Murder is always a tragedy, but when it involves people who are trying to extend kindness it is always such a painful blow. They have three grown children; please pray for them if you think of it.

One of our dorm guys was at home during the break, and had a perforated bowel. His parents are stationed in Tanzania, and the hospital he was at had two people to a bed.

Eighth grade. Fighting for your life. And doing it while sharing a bed with a total stranger. It boggles the mind. He is going to make it, but the reality of being remote hits home again.

There was some good news. One of our students was accepted at Princeton. When I heard the news, I thought about the path I went down to become the college advisor.

When I was in the states, I worked for three companies that went belly up in the course of 16 months. I got a job at a company selling publishing to universities. It was not an especially good job; the owner was an eccentric man... I was so gun shy after the other companies going under that I tried to make it work.

After my first year at the company, I was consistently the top performer for many years. It did not make it easier for me at the company, and I began to try to find another job. I couldn't find anything that would pay near what I was making, and so I endured lots of humiliations for many years. I was up for a job that received 600 resumes, and it came down to me and one other person, and when I didn't get the job, I can still reach back and feel the disappointment and hurt I felt.

The job brought me to the campuses of almost 800 colleges. I learned much about colleges, and the quality differences between them. I didn't enjoy the company, but I truly enjoyed the college environment.

I absolutely love what I'm doing now. Talking to kids about college is one of the most satisfying things I've ever done.

And the reason I bring some value to it is because of those eight tough years. All those years that I thought were a waste brought me back to technology, and then being fairly knowledgeable about colleges. And a young man from a small school that struggles with baboons on its campus is going to Princeton.

You can trust His plan for your life.

At the marriage seminar we recently attended, we were eating under the stars, and there was a dance floor. It is against RVA policy to dance, but I asked the pastor for a special exception, and he granted it. It was a beautiful evening, warm with a nice breeze.

I asked Katie if she would dance with me, and she very seriously replied `Yes I will.' We walked to the dance floor, she put her feet on top of my feet, and she looked up at me with a smile that was brighter than all the stars above us.

There are moments that are so special that they get you through the other stuff.

And now we get to the other stuff. I tend to shy away from asking for prayer in these letters, mostly because I figure that anyone who is reading them KNOWS how much I need prayer, and they do it without asking.

But we are in trouble with the visas for the twins. Between the Kenyan government and the U.S. embassy, we have made twenty trips into town (three hours to get there and back) to try to get all the paperwork we need. We got told this week that the US Embassy was going to deny the visa we applied for.

It really doesn't make any sense to deny it, but we are now in circumstances that we were trying to avoid by beginning this process in November. There is no way for us to get the other visa in time; some of the things they require take months, and we return to the states in mid-July.

So I am asking for prayer for two things:

1. Pray for a miracle and that we are granted the visa we originally sought. It will take the hand of God.
2. I want to go into this believing that God hasn't forgotten us, and He has set this up to change things in me that need to be changed. I want to embrace this, not rage against it, and model the proper response to my children and dorm kids. I want to be more like Jesus, and I think this is a tool designed by Him to accomplish it.

I trust His plan for my life. I just want to act like I do.

Your pal,

Steve

Your Pal, Steve

The Power and the Glory
— *May 12, 2004*

The visa situation wasn't going well. We had started the process in November, and chased down every rabbit they asked us to chase We had received an email from the embassy at the end of April that included:

Your below is incorrect, and I do not appreciate being quoted on things I did not say. If you fail to provide the required documents, the case will be denied.

And:

In my experience, petitioners often hear what they want to hear, and this case is an example. The below is a misstatement of facts.

So we made another trip into the Embassy, and we asked what we needed. The gentlemen who wrote the above wasn't available, so we talked to someone who didn't know anything about what we were trying to do. We started over with her, but she told us what we needed; a letter from a government official who would say that we had had legal custody of the twins for two years.

We knew someone in the government we had worked with in the adoption. She still worked for the government, and told us that she would be glad to write the letter for us. She told us that she would write it by the end of the week and drop it off at the orphanage.

The end of the week came. No letter.

We called her on Friday, and she said that we could pick it up from the orphanage on Monday. We were going into town anyway, so we said that would be great. There was flooding in Nairobi, so the usual one hour trip took three hours. We called the orphanage. No letter.

We called Margaret, and asked if we could pick it up. She said yes. We asked her where her office was. She said `I cannot tell you. Go to the Insurance Plaza and call me from there.'

At that point, although it wasn't far, traffic was so weird that we decided to get a cab. We were blessed; we got a nice big guy who wasn't afraid to go wherever he needed to go to get us there. At one point, we were in the middle of an intersection and it looked like a bad movie; cars were going in every direction. He just kept pushing until we got to the insurance plaza. We called Margaret.

>Margaret: Just stand on the corner. I will come out and get you.
>Us: Ok.

We waited about ten minutes. We were afraid it looked like a drug buy, but Margaret finally came by with the letter. We read it and thanked her, and she ran back to a meeting.

We were thrilled, and after thanking our cab driver for braving the drive back to our car, began the drive home. We had to go through water that was almost up to our car windows, but after a few close calls, we got home.

We had planned to call the Embassy the next day and try to schedule an appointment, but we got a shocking call at 7:30 the next morning. We had called the Embassy. We had called the Embassy dozens of times and left dozens of messages that had never been returned. Our contact person had been gratuitously rude to us on several occasions, and had written the emails referenced above.

And he called to apologize. He told us that our hearts were in the right place, and he was sorry for giving us the wrong information about the agency he had told us to contact. I read the letter we had received, and he said that was great.

We got word today that our visas were approved.

There are two wonderful things that occurred through this process:

We asked people to pray, because we didn't know what else to do anymore. So many people wrote and offered to call their elected officials, to write letters, to do anything they could to help. We were overwhelmed by that.

But what we saw was that prayer changed this guy's heart. He went from being antagonistic to being kind, and the only thing that changed was that we asked people to pray. God changed his heart.

We were determined to try to embrace the process, and while we were at the Embassy to drop off our paperwork, we saw a young American couple who were there trying to get out of the country as fast as they could because he was self employed and they had been in Kenyan for months trying to adopt a child.

Because of what we had been through, we could tell him where to go and who to talk to. We have good friends that have come back to Kenya to adopt another child, and we think that we can save them weeks of time because we know some of the pitfalls to avoid.

We are so grateful for the visas, but we are more grateful for friends who would stand with us and pray in our hour of need. And I am most grateful for beginning to learn how to embrace His process, and seeing the fruit that results from that.

We have seen the power of prayer, and the strength of His glory. Thank you for helping us to find Him in the midst of all of this.

Your pal,

Steve

Your Pal, Steve

Right Hand Fork, Left Hand Knife: Fine Dining in the Eighth Grade

— *June 1, 2004*

Kenya put their tax forms out on April 20. Taxes were due April 30. When people protested, they made a ruling that explains much about this country. *Taxes* were still due on the 30th, but the *forms* weren't due until *June* 30th.

We had the annual Eighth Grade Formal recently. It's always funny, and it's always sad that the parents don't get to see their guys clean up so nice. One guy was so scared about being incorrect that he wrote on his hands: RIGHT HAND FORK, LEFT HAND KNIFE. One guy was so excited about getting to sit with the girl he liked that he was bouncing off the walls for days before. When he got back to the dorm, he was pretty subdued:

Me: What's the matter?

Them: I was so excited when I found out I got to sit next to her, but after two minutes, I ran out of things to say.

Me: What did you do?

Them: I looked the other way the rest of the night.

It's easy to forget how hard it is to be an eighth grader, and how awkward that age can be. Sometimes, I think that the bravest people I know are eighth graders at this school; to go through that interesting stage of life away from your parents would be so hard.

We get back to the states on July 17th. It is a long journey; we leave at 10:30 at night from Nairobi, and fly eight hours to London. Then we gather all of our luggage and go to the other airport in London to sit for about five hours. Then we fly ten hours to Dallas. The last time, we were all excited about getting home. Lots of our friends came to the airport to meet us; it was a special memory.

This time we will be traveling with the dynamic duo, who hate crowds and new things and not getting enough sleep, so we are going to try to slip into town as quietly as we can, and once we get our sea legs back, we hope to get to see everyone. We will be living in Bedford Texas for the year.

My hope is to not work until September. We are all tired, and we will have lots of work to get everyone readjusted to America. The older boys have not been in the United States since August of 2001. They missed 9/11. Reality TV, McGriddles and so much more. And they have changed; JT is wearing contacts, playing rugby, climbed Mt. Kenya and rafted the Nile. Matthew is comfortable with shillings or dollars, the piano or the drums, and English and Swahili.

If you wish to continue to support the feeding program, any monies that come in after May 2004 will not be used until August 2005. If you can continue to support us while we are on home assignment, we would appreciate it. We understand if you can't, but if you can, that would be helpful. Our largest supporter has not been able to support us for the last several months, so we will need to raise additional support when we are back. I'm not sure what kind of job I will be able to get for just one year, but I will get something. But we are going to try hard to spend part of this time at home resting; we are tired.

RVA has asked that the feeding program would cease while we are away. All of us work more than full time jobs, and adding this would be a distraction to a new staff member. The staff members who have been here for awhile have their own projects, and most everyone is stretched pretty thin. The feeding program takes a lot of time, and it is probably for the best that it takes a rest for a year.

So it was quite bittersweet to be on the last delivery for a year. Headmasters got quite emotional as we told them we would have to curtail the program for a year. I had to explain that there was no more money in the fund, and I needed to be there to supervise, but they have seen the fruit in this program, and as I listened to grown men telling me about children running that didn't run after noon because they would normally be too tired, I thought: burn this into your heart. Let it hurt.

In the spirit of full disclosure, I should inform you that I received a kickback from this program, and I'm not giving it back, no matter what.

I couldn't give it back anyway. My name is on it. In fact, it is so specific it says `A Gift for Steve Peifer' right on it.

And I'm not sure anyone else would want a purse with my name on it.

Yes, a purse. Why, I don't know. But it was made by a parent at one of the schools we feed, and although I try hard to discourage that kind of thing (there is nothing harder in the world than receiving stuff from people who have nothing) what could I do?

I'm not even sure what to DO with a purse. But I do have one now. So there you go, and back off.

We went to Kenton this week. This is the school that has started having afternoon classes for the first time since we started providing lunches because before the lunches, the kids didn't have the energy to handle the afternoon classes. It is very remote, and almost impossibly beautiful, surrounded by large green hills. It was also so poor it would take your breath away.

It is so poor. But they had some entertainment for us. They had a dance troupe, and a young man who played a homemade xylophone. At closer range, I could see it was made with discarded fence posts.

And it sounded so great. It was the most amazing thing, this little kid playing this wonderful music on this junky homemade instrument, and I thought how it would have been his right to think `I can't do anything on this piece of junk' and not try. But he knew what was in his hand.

I have pondered this for days. What is really in my hand? If I looked at what I had differently, would it change the way I lived my life? If I knew what I really had, how would I change?

One last thing. The woman that opens the computer center gets there at 7, and from 7:30 until school starts at 8 10 kids can use the computers for thirty minutes.

Kids have been arriving at 5am to get in line to get an extra 30 minutes on the computers. If I ever take things for granted again, you have permission to slap me hard.

The programs are bearing such fruit. Please help us grow them. It would be wonderful to expand the feeding program to cover 100 schools, and build 24 more computer centers. May I ask you if you could ask your church or corporation if I could speak to them? I need some larger venues in order to fund such expansion, and I don't know how to do it without your help. Can you help us help these kids?

Will you look and see what is in your hand?

And no, you can't have my purse.

Your pal,

Steve

PS. One of my best and oldest friends in the world (since sixth grade) has a book coming out in July, and I want to do a shameless plug for it. The name of the book is the Millennium Matrix by Rex Miller, and I had the privilege of reading the draft copy. I read it with a mixture of wonder and depression. It will make you think and ponder so many issues in our society. It depressed me because I wondered how someone who went to the same junior high and high school could be so much smarter than me. Here is the link:

http://www.josseybass.com/WileyCDA/WileyTitle/productCd-0787962678.html

Why I Like Momma Better; the Daughter Reveals the Tragic Secret
— June 18, 2004

Truth be told, I was the older boys' favorite when they were younger. But that is not the case with the dynamic duo, who favor Nancy to a staggering degree. I'm not threatened by this; it is a sign of their high intelligence.

However, I discovered WHY Nancy is the favorite, and I must admit to seeing a sense of relief. Katie and Ben are on a blistering pace to complete toilet training; I am now hoping they will be toilet trained before THEY retire. But I had Katie on top of the potty, and she asked for Momma.

> Me: Why do you want Momma?
>
> Katie: Momma wipes better.
>
> Me: How does someone wipe better?
>
> Katie: Momma wipes twice.

There you have it, and any suggestions on techniques can go to my dear friend Rex Miller at rex@spencer-furniture.com (who has an amazing book coming out next month) and is probably looking for ideas for the sequel.

One of my favorite parts of life right now is how much the twins love their big brothers. When JT leaves for school, he makes a big show of walking to the door and saying `BYE!' The twins immediately yell `KISS' and he walks back and kisses them goodbye. The way they interact is one of my favorite parts of life.

They had the official opening ceremony for the computer center on Friday. Like many Kenyan traditions, it was confusing and exhilarating at the same time. There were probably a thousand people in attendance.

They had a `tent' set up (it was some maize bags tied together) , and a car battery hooked up to a sound system, and an obsequious announcer who would say things like `Steve Peifer is now walking towards us' who had generally inane things to say throughout the afternoon, which made it funnier to be there.

The first thing was to plant a tree, which made me miss my friend Mark Buhler, who did so much to instill tree planting in Kenya. After that, it was time to see lots of entertainment. Nancy and I got to sit on the first row, next to the MP (member of Parliament) who was funny and charming.

They decorated us with something that I can only compare to a Hawaiian lei with an ornament you might put on an ugly Christmas tree.

Then the stupid moment hit.

Some of the children were doing a dance, and they invited the MP to and dance with them. She knew the moves, and the kids loved it.

Then they asked me.

Long time readers are familiar with my dancing issues. Instead of gracefully waving them off, I had this weird thought: Maybe I could pull this off.

And I got up there and danced. And hundreds of kids starting screaming `Can you teach ME how to dance like that?' For a moment, Africa and America were as one.

Actually, when I got up there, for some mysterious reason, the only dance I could think of was to do something like I saw on Hullabaloo (and if you don't know what that is, say a prayer of thanks)

They all LAUGHED at me.

There were lots and lots of speeches. The MC introduced each speaker with `the hope that their worthy remarks will remain brief.' This was not to be, but the speakers were good, with some surprising things to say.

Many people noted that until the computer center was built, they felt isolated and unknown. Three different people said that they couldn't understand why this center was built in the middle of nowhere. But they all said they didn't think they were in the middle of nowhere anymore.

But the best thing the headmaster said was that the ones most excited were not the parents or the present students; it was the younger students, because they could see that they had a future.

What a gift you have given to them.

Walter and I went through the center while we were there, looking for structural issues, power difficulties or any other problems. We couldn't find any. We had wanted to make sure it was right before we continued.

We received notice of funding for the second center this week. There will be issues as to where it goes, but another school is going to get a chance.

The world can change if we want it to change. We can be passive, and allow what has occurred to continue, or we can say `No more hungry children and no more children without opportunity.'

It's our choice, and our opportunity.

Your pal,

Steve

P.S. We will leave for the states four weeks from today!

You Have Become an African Man
— June 26, 2004

I never expected to become friends with Margaret, but I'm grateful for it nonetheless. I began to know her when I first started buying maize and beans. I went to market myself, and could never beat her prices. She was a brilliant negotiator, and I soon started buying most of my beans from her.

When the pastor I was dealing with was transferred, Margaret started going with me to the schools. Her husband is a pastor, and because of his schedule, he asked that Margaret would go with me.

She has a merry laugh, doesn't suffer fools, and every time we hit a pothole, she yells `Oh my God, save me' which makes long trips fun and eventful.

Last week, I was delayed picking her up, and she got into the car and said `You have become an African man.'

I thought `Was it the dance moves that made her think that? My innate coolness?`

No.

Kenyan men are always late.

I'm still holding out for the dance moves.

We took our last trip out to Kenton. The kids are so happy and so poor. Their clothes are in the worst shape I've seen.

But we were able to tell the headmaster that it is likely that the new computer center will be built at his school.

He just looked at me and looked at the hill and looked at me and looked at the hill. He didn't say anything for the longest time. Sometimes silence can be the most eloquent thing you can say.

We will be back in the US in less than three weeks for a whole year. When I think about why I will miss this place, I think about Erik.

Erik is a golden boy. Good looking, great basketball player, lead in the musical, some of the highest scores on the SAT2 in the history of the school.

His dad is a surgeon who gives up millions to be out here. Erik dates the prom queen, or at least she probably would be if we had a prom.

Anyway, we had cafeteria duty last week, and for the first time ever, they had little bags of chips that were probably past the due date (because that is when they are affordable). It hadn't happened before in the cafeteria.

And Erik walked in, and went `WOW!! Bags of chips!!' He was so elated, and it's one of the reasons I love this place.

Where else does the coolest kid on the block get thrilled with a bag of stale chips?

Your pal,

Steve

PS. We are inviting all of our friends in the DFW area to join us at Milwaukee Joe's on Friday July 23rd at 7:30. Come enjoy the best ice cream in America and marvel at how I have gained so much weight without access to any of it!

Will I Still be Three in America? The Twins Contemplate the Journey to America
— July 12, 2004

Have you ever met a hero and made a fool of yourself?

A few months ago, I was leaving a school which has one textbook for every seven children, and I was in a rather foul mood. An official government procession went by, and by law, you must pull over to the side of the road, stop your engine and get out of your car.

And I counted over 15 new Mercedes.

I had one of my hitting the steering wheel of my car drives home, but I read something the next day in the newspaper that spoke the truth about the Kenyan budget. Sunny (the journalist at the newspaper) was so on the money that I had to write him and thank him for articulating what I felt in a way far more eloquent than I would ever be able to.

And another unlikely friendship in Kenya was born. Sunny is a Hindu who is not fond of current American policy, and perhaps has some distrust of all Americans. I am probably the poster child for the ugly American.

But we found a bond in our view of economic policy in Kenya. Week after week, he spoke the truth in a country that doesn't always reward the truth, and fairly recently, would punish it severely.

And I would write to him to comment, and we began to forge an email friendship. We had both been consultants, both worked in technology, and both had a love for Kenya and a deep sadness for the things that drag it down.

He asked me once about what I was doing, and I told him about the computer center and the feeding program. He asked if he could visit sometime, and we set a time.

It was going to be a great day for him to visit. We were going to award prizes for kids who typed the fastest and the most accurate. After three months, children who had never seen a computer before were typing 50WPM with 95% accuracy.

I wanted Sunny to see the project, because he has been in technology, and I have been out of it for so long that I don't trust my own judgment sometimes. He was complimentary and helpful with suggestions.

But I was like a fan boy at a Star Trek Convention who asks Mr. Spock questions like `In episode 23, you began a sentence in the first 15 minutes and had an unusually long pause. WHY?'

I was saying things to Sunny like:

> Me: `You know the column you wrote about the effects on regressive tax policy on economic growth?'
> Sunny: Yes?
> Me: `It was awesome.'

The twins are not exactly sure about all this America business. Not much has gotten through, although we have tried hard to tell them about all the wonders of the USA. We have had several discussions like this:

> Me: You will have so much fun in America!!
> Them: Will Lauren be in America?
> Me: No. But you will make LOTS of friends in America.
> Them: Will I still be three in America?
> Me: Yes!!

Many of you have asked what our plans are for our year in America. We hope to begin by getting some rest. The end of school is so busy and so stressful, and when you add to that trying to pack everything you have and storing it away in a different place for a year, and you add three years of 24x7 dorm duties and adopting twins and everything else, you might come upon me and say `He is a bucket of chuckles.'

But you probably wouldn't.

So after a few weeks of rest, we are going to shop for clothing. It would be in bad taste to tell you the state of repair that my underwear is in, but my friend Chris would say that it is held together with baling wire and spit. We want the older boys to get reacclimated to the states, and try to see America through the eyes of our three year olds, who have never been to the US before.

RVA has given me encouragement to get certified in college guidance, so I am going to take a series of classes online through UCLA to get further training in that area. The goal the Lord has put on my heart is to come back to Kenya in a year with enough funding for 25 computer centers and 100 schools being fed.

In addition, our own support level is low enough that we would not be allowed to return until it is at our mission approved level, so we need to seek out new support. I hope to find some kind of work once the older boys start school in the middle of August. And, someone is planning to publish a collection of our emails for a book, which still amazes me.

It has been a wonderful three years. Someone asked me: `What accomplishment are you most proud of?' Upon consideration, I realized it was something most of you don't even know about. I decided that I needed to be home on Tuesday mornings and Thursday afternoons so Nancy could work at the library. I've always been so driven in any kind of work situation (not that I was necessarily successful or hard working, but I found my identity in working) that laying it down was very difficult for me.

Recognizing that Nancy's work was as or more important than mine, and that I needed more time with the twins doesn't sound deep or spiritual, but it was the eternal moment for me.

I know this has been lengthy, but I wanted to end with thanks to all of you. It would be difficult to sum up what you all have meant to us without getting sappy or weepy, both of which are things I like to avoid. What comes to mind is an old TV show called The Invaders. The plot was about this guy who discovers that aliens have landed and are plotting to take over the world.

And no one believes him. Worse, no one cares.

In you, we have found people who would weep with us in what we have seen and experienced in Kenya. There are many people who are bored to death with what we write about, and I can't say I blame them.

But you have stood with us, and often times, it was an email from someone who gave us the fuel to continue the fight, and to be encouraged in it.

I still go back to the end of the TV show. On the last show, the guy is seated at a table with a small group of people. The stern voiced narrator says

`Finally, he has discovered allies. Those who also know. Those who believe.' And the guy looks at the group of people at his table, and he weeps.

Thank you for all you have done for us, and what you have done for the people of Kenya. You all have made a difference in so many people's lives. You have been a voice for the voiceless. You have given hope to the hopeless.

Please don't take this wrong, but when I think of you guys, sometimes I just weep

Your pal,

Steve

PS. We are inviting all of our friends in the DFW area to join us at Milwaukee Joe's on Friday July 23rd at 7:30. Come enjoy the best ice cream in America and marvel at how I have gained so much weight without access to any of it!

Ain't Them Cute: The Twins Conquer America
— *October 20, 2004*

Whenever you have an international trip, there is always one incident that makes you remember it; it happened when we went through security in Nairobi. JT's carry-on was his saxophone, and when they opened it up, there was an interesting conversation:

> Security: What is this?
> JT: It is a saxophone.
> Security: What is a saxophone?
> JT: It is a musical instrument.
> Security: You must play it in order for us to believe you.

So at ten o'clock in the evening, JT did a song for the security agents. I suspect they knew what it was, but they were looking for some entertainment. JT got into it; it was fun to see him get into the spirit of it. He is a different kid than he was three years ago.

The only thing that connected with Katie about what we told her about America was that there were nice people who you could call on the phone and they would bring pizza to your house. It is a long flight; almost 24 hours of travel and you begin at 10:30 in the evening, so we were tired when we finally arrived.

We ordered a pizza, and I wish you could have seen her face when a nice man came and left us pizza. For the next three days, when someone used the phone, Katie would come running and yell `Pizza!'

After a day or so, we ventured out to a grocery store. Matthew yelled and we all came running. `Oreos! Double-stuff Oreos! Green Oreos! Fudge covered Oreos! Vanilla Oreos!' And as he continued down his list, JT started shoveling them into the cart. If you ever saw this many kinds of Oreos in Kenya, you would buy them, because they wouldn't be there next time. We explained they would still be there next week, and we realized that there would be some readjustment issues this time around.

Or just plain adjustment issues. Ben and Kate were fascinated with doorbells and ceiling fans and carpet and just about everything. One day the three of us were out for a walk and a fire engine went by. They started crying and wanted to be held; it took me awhile to remember that they had never heard a siren or seen a fire engine before. Now it is one of their favorite things, but it took awhile.

Brief updates on all of us:

Nancy: Nancy had been sick for five months in Kenya. She didn't get better for the first month we were back, so we had her tested for TB. We were so glad when she tested negative, and that some concentrated rest has her feeling more like herself. She is almost all the way back. She went up to Chicago last week because her father went into the hospital. Despite his being in the hospital they had some great one on one time with him. We are grateful that he is doing better.

JT: JT is playing football after three years of playing rugby. He has access to a great weight room and coach, so he is getting bigger and taller. Both he and Matthew have been blessed by the ability to return to the school they grew up in. It has made the adjustment so much easier. Besides football, he is in a band called No Zebra, which consists of three guitars, a drummer, a saxophone and …

a tuba.

Matthew: Matthew loved swimming in July and August. He is continuing piano lessons and started drum lessons. He is hoping to make the basketball team. He loves riding his bike on flat smooth roads.

Katie and Ben: They are fascinated by America; by all the driving, by garage trucks, by the wonder of McDonalds. We went to a Mexican restaurant, and Ben stood up with both hands clutching chips, almost overcome by the thrill of all the food. Katie was at swimming lessons, and afterwards was using the hand dryer. Ben told her that her hands were already dry, and she informed him that she was trying to get the wrinkles out.

Me: I had a great fear of coming back and someone saying something ugly to the twins. The twins and I were at a hardware store, and some big redneck looking guy in a bib overall kept looking at us. He came over, and I had my hand on a wrench, and I was going to hit him if he said something unkind to my babies. He looked at me and looked at them and said `Ain't them cute?'.

I'm working for a consulting company for the smartest human on the planet, which has been intimidating and inspiring in equal measures. I'm taking several classes to get certified in college counseling. I've gotten to speak in Houston and Connecticut trying to increase funding for the computer centers and the feeding program.

The saying among missionaries in Africa is when Kenyan ice cream starts to taste good to you, it's time to go on furlough. I am eating far too much of it, as you can tell if you see me.

I think it was the master, Neil Diamond, who said:

> LA's fine, the sun shines most the time

> And the feeling is laid back

> Palm trees grow and the rents are low but you know I keep thinking about

> Making my way back

> I'm New York City born and raised but now days I live between two shores

> LA's fine but it ain't home

> New York's home but it ain't mine no mo

We can forget about the rest of the song when Neil talks to chairs and frogs and focus on the feeling that we don't quite fit in anymore. We're grateful to be back for a year, but it has been a challenge in some ways.

We went by the cemetery, and stood by the gravesite. Stephen would have been six, and you wonder what would have happened if he had lived. And as we wondered, Ben and Katie sat by his gravestone.

It was one of the most bittersweet moments in our lives.

We are back until August. We would love to hear from you, and we would appreciate it if you updated your mailing addresses. We had computer blues in Kenya, and have had to recreate lots of our list.

Thanks for all your kindness to us. May He bless you.

Your pal,

Steve

So! Been eating, have you? Six Months in America
— *February 24, 2005*

It's been an interesting year back in the United States. I'm not a terribly insightful person, but I think I've figured out one thing about America.

The first week we were back in the states I took Ben and Kate to Wal-Mart. As we walked through, with their eyes almost popping out of their sockets, I saw something that I hadn't seen three years ago.

Wal-Mart was selling three thousand dollar TV's. I was so amazed at this that I just stopped and looked. A salesperson thought I might be a prospect, and they began giving me all sorts of information. They didn't appreciate my question: `Does Gilligan get off the island if you watch it on a 3k machine?'

They didn't think it was funny either, but what struck me was seeing an ad for the same TV several months later, and the price had been reduced to $2400.00 and I thought `What a good deal.'

America just wears you down. They hit you with ad after ad after ad and after a while you start to believe everything they tell you. Even overreaching TVs.

But we have enjoyed being back. When people haven't seen you for awhile, the usual response is `You look great.' The most common response I've had since I've been back is `So! Been eating have you?'

We go to North Carolina to spend Thanksgiving with my sister and her husband, and while we are there, JT and I go visit Wake Forest. He won't be able to visit colleges next year, so this is our opportunity. Two days before we arrive, we arrange to meet two graduates from RVA who are studying at Wake Forest. Two days before we arrive, she is awarded the Rhodes scholarship. Only 37 are awarded a year; as far as I know, it is the first time a RVA student has ever received the Rhodes. One thing I am sure of: it is a GOOD thing to visit a college and be the high school counselor of the school that provided the student who won a Rhodes two days previously. I've met with lots of colleges, but never had a meeting quite like that before.

JT tells me he is the only person in his class who won't receive a car when he turns 16. I ask him if that is hard on him; he tells me he is fine. (Truth be known, it was harder on me) The NEXT day, I get an email from an old friend from the gym who asks if JT would like her 1988 Honda with 215,000 miles. It has been well maintained and is far nicer than we could have hoped for.

A few months later, I'm sitting at the repair shop waiting on the verdict for the new radiator the Honda needs. I'm discouraged. I get a phone call AS I'M WAITING from a friend who tells me that when I stayed with one of his relatives during a speaking engagement I had really impacted her life. It is difficult to stay discouraged.

I pick up the car and can't get it out of first gear. I return it to the garage, discouraged. The mechanic says he will take it out for a drive to check it. While he does, I meet a pilot who invites me to his Bible study. The car returns without a problem and I gain several new friends.

Whoever Ben sneezes, I tell him he is Sneezey McGee. He informs me one day that his name is HAPPY McGee.

I wake up Katie to begin a trip to go to Iowa and Minnesota. She puts her arms around me and whispers `Daddy, I was dreaming it was snowing.' It snows up north, and she is so thrilled.

Matthew doesn't make the basketball team. He is sad, but I remind him that he hasn't held a basketball since the previous season. He gets to be the manager, and they allow him to work out with the team. He is faithful, and someone leaves the team. The coach says that `I need your heart' and Matthew gets on the team. In his first game, his teammates cheer for him to get into the game and he plays the final two minutes. A father couldn't script sowing and reaping any better than this.

Nancy has gotten well again. Months of walking pneumonia had fatigued her, but months of rest have brought her back to health.

I get the following email on a discouraging day:

Dear Mr. Peifer,

The very first day I came up to talk to you about colleges you described me as the driver of a very nice Jaguar and that I was happy to cruise along at 40mph without caring what I had under my hood. I believe you were right.

Today, after much stress and work, I believe I've found the accelerator.

At 11:06 pm my time I received an email from Stanford University. The first three words were "Dear Greg, Congratulations..." I thought you should know because I honestly believe you set me on my track to my acceptance to Stanford University. With your passion for me to succeed and your goading to press further, I've been accepted to one of the premier universities of the world.

Thank you from the depths of my heart

We have made our reservations to return to Kenya. We leave the United States on August 9th. Time is flying by, although the next three weeks will be interesting trying to finish up three classes! (I'm getting certified in college counseling while I'm back)

I've sent as an attachment our information about supporting us when we return to Kenya. If you received this in the mail, it's the same thing, but there are lots of people we don't have a snail address for.

Nancy went to visit her father in Arizona a few weekends ago, and I knew I wouldn't get any work done, so I took Ben and Katie to their first movie in a theater. They asked a lot of questions before we went in about the lights being dark. When we finally went in, they were fascinated by the lights on the ground. We decided to go around the entire theater and count ALL the lights. After that, we sat down and they were thrilled by the rocking seats.

The lights dimmed, and they both grabbed my hands. Then the movie started. So many children's movies wink at adults, but the new Winnie the Pooh movie is aimed straight at 3 year olds; preferably three year olds who aren't media savvy.

They loved it. And I sat in that theater, and could feel cynicism just fall off of me as I thanked God for the chance to see the earth through their eyes.

When you do, it can be such a beautiful world.

Your pal,

Steve

PS Please forgive the following link, but I couldn't quite resist: http://www.neildiamond.com/

I've heard worse: Enthralling audiences across America
— *April 8, 2005*

When missionaries would come to my church, I would suddenly remember that I had important work to do in the nursery. I thought they were dweebs with bad haircuts who whined about money.

As my older sister would say, `There you go.'

The wonder of the principle of sowing and reaping is that between work and school, I've been speaking at churches all over the place in the last few months. We are scheduled to return to Kenya August 9th, and I've had the chance to speak at several groups and churches.

People have generally been very kind. One old friend, however, brought his family to hear me in Springfield, Illinois and his stepson had the agonized face of a teenager who did NOT want to be there and had been dragged against his will. Because he looked so unhappy, I felt like it would be helpful to let him know how horrible it was going to be. I told him that I had been arrested for boring the life out of people in three different states, and that I was tired tonight, so it could get really bad. Afterwards, I asked him how I did, and he gave me the highest praise he was capable of giving:

`I've heard worse.'

I have learned one important lesson in public speaking. When speaking in Dallas, do NOT follow one of the coaches of the Dallas Cowboys. Some friends said they wanted to do a fundraising banquet for us, and they would handle all of it. They managed to get one of the coaches, and then told us we got to speak AFTER the coach.

This is Dallas, where many people believe that the Cowboys' gas could be sold as perfume at Macys. I believed it myself in the early 90's, and regularly purchased it in great quantities.

To follow a Cowboys coach was as nerve racking as any speaking I have ever done. Since he was a genuinely nice man with a real heart for what we are trying to do, it was hard to be anything but be grateful and hope that people would stay around for what we had to say. People were kind and generous, but I still wake up and wonder if the evening really happened.

Brief updates on all of us:

Nancy went down to Austin to attend a library convention. It was a good break for her, and she got lots of ideas for the library, as well as time with her best friend. Since the children all clustered at the door anxiously awaiting her return, I'm not sure the bonding time I had hoped for the rest of us occurred.

JT was truly enjoying track and excelling at it when his knee began to bother him. He had to have a cyst removed from his knee, and some repair work done besides. It was much more painful than he expected, and it has been discouraging for him. But the wonder of my oldest son is that he finds new things to occupy his time. He discovered a scholarship that he has applied for that is unique. If you attend your formal in a duct tape suit, you can win a 5k scholarship. Because he is on crutches, he didn't think he would make the funniest of dates, so he gave himself to this project with a vengeance. He reports that all wanted to have their picture taken with him, and it was a bonding night for him with his classmates.

JT has started a new project. We encouraged both the older boys to come up with a project for Kenya; that they are there for reasons besides being related to Nancy and I. His project is to build a greenhouse at every school we provide lunches for. He drew up the plans, did the costing, and has come up with an idea that can really help Kenya start to replant. We are proud of him.

Matthew is running track, and improving every single day. He got his braces off, and has celebrated by chewing gum in his sleep. His project is to try to get Happy Meal toys shipped to Kenya for us to give to the kids in the hospital and orphanages. His line is : Lost the Need? Plant a Seed!

Ben and Kate are enjoying swimming lessons and half price books. They go to a Mother's Day Out for a morning a week, and come home with stories about the infamous Kevin, who never obeys. One shudders to wonder what stories Kevin can tell.

I can tell two stories. One of the best people I know, and one of best friends I've ever had is a man named Jeff. He has a fine family and works hard. If you don't look deep, you see nothing out of the ordinary. But if you have been lucky enough to look deep, you will see an extraordinary man. My distance away helped me see the miracle he is.

Because I went to Africa, I get pats on the back and the occasional pulpit to share. But I'm the same guy I always was, and I was unique before I ever went to Africa. I needed someone to see that. My suggestion to American Christians is to see the wonder in all our brothers and sisters, and give lots of room to celebrate it.

I keep saying it, but there is nothing special about a missionary. What is special is finding out what He has called you to, and doing it. Which means there is a special story in all of us that needs to be sought out, and given a forum. I appreciate that I have one, but I long for the day when Christians see what the special thing that God has put in all of us.

I've been so grateful for the opportunity to speak across the country. I spoke in Ohio one morning, and then traveled several hours to speak at another church in the evening. It was cold, and I was curious to see who might turn up.

There were about 15 people who showed up, and they were kind beyond kind. I shared my current favorite scripture: `For I know the plans I have for you' says the Lord. `Plans for good and not for evil, to give you a future and a hope.'

But what I will never forget is a little girl who came up to me with a box she had decorated. She told me that she had read the emails about the hungry kids, and so she had decided to go door to door to collect pennies for them.

She told me she wanted to give them hope.

Little kids helping little kids is about as good as it gets.

Your pal,

Steve

PS. We are still looking for opportunities to speak, and we are glad to announce that we will be sharing at our church, Woodland Heights Baptist Church 3712 Central Drive, Bedford, TX 76021-2653 (817)571-7884 at both the 8:15 and 10:50 services on April 17th.

Your Pal, Steve

The Ultimate Sacrifice
— *April 29, 2005*

The letters has been storming in. Hundreds, lo even THOUSANDS, wondering what I will do. People asking `Will he not go back to Kenya now? Will he come later?'

And the calls. The volume has prevented any of them from getting through, but I imagine people saying `How is it possible that you could still be going?'

But yet, somehow I am. People will look at me and weep and start chanting `What a NOBLE man.'

I'm sure you know the story, but for the very few, here is the chronicle:

Our flight to Kenya leaves on AUGUST 9th.

Neil Diamond comes to Dallas on OCTOBER 14th.

And as unbelievably as it sounds, I WILL be on that flight.

I've always wanted to be an example in my faith. Finally, I have the opportunity to make the ULTIMATE sacrifice.

Sometimes I even amaze myself.

Nancy and I spoke at our church last week for both services. I love my wife, I love looking at my wife, but after listening to her give the same talk for two services, I have a new empathy for all political wives. I tried to gaze at her with an adoring look, but it's HARD to be Laura Bush.

When we return to Kenya in about three months, it will be easy to say what we enjoyed the most, besides seeing family and friends.

It has been the changing of seasons. Seeing winter become spring has been a thrill for the twins to be sure, but it has been wonderful for all of us. Ben and Kate have never seen a real spring before, and the rest of us have reacted like we never have before. It has been such an unexpected gift.

I have a tradition of watching the Final Four with some rude friends from Kansas, and they say unkind things to me all evening. I, of course, pray for their souls and their taste in basketball teams. We hadn't seen the Final Four since 2001.

But this year, after the game, we stayed and talked and talked. It was just hard to let it go. When I finally left, I drove a block and it hit me; I won't be insulted during a Final Four in America until 2011.

Part of my practicum for my degree in college counseling involved taking the SAT. I was thrilled to receive a perfect score on the verbal, and dismayed that my math score was so low that they recommended that I refrain from driving. I'm learning so much, but the clock is ticking so fast.

We were in a daze for the first few months we got back, and already it's almost time to go back.

I'm not ready to go, and I can't wait to get there.

Your pal,

Steve

PS. Nancy and I have our 20th anniversary in June. Any cheap suggestions for a getaway? For some reason, Nancy has rejected by suggestion that Omaha is lovely this time of year and coincidentally is the kick off start to the Neil Diamond tour.

The End of the Dream and the Birth of Hope
— May 17, 2005

The goal was 25 computer centers and 100 schools being fed. It's getting late in the game, but we had one more big chance. Some friends invited us to share after their church service at their large church in MN. I had this hope that the right people would hear the message, and we would hit the goals.

And then the pastor, who had been at the church for 17 years, announced he was resigning from the pulpit to go on the mission field. He was going to have a meeting right after the service; the same time as our meeting. I leaned over to our host and said `I want to go to his meeting too!'

So did everyone else. We had a few people show up, but I realized that there would be no way that this church would close the gap. And the most wonderful thing happened to me: I felt covered in His peace like I have never felt before. It was a wonderful weekend of fellowship with dear friends that was refreshing and inspiring.

My dream ended, but He birthed a hope in me. I don't have a clue how big this thing should get or will get, but my hope is in Him.

We've attached our most recent snail mail because we don't have snail for everyone.

We also wanted to let you know that we are going to be at Colleyville Christian Fellowship this Sunday, May 22nd from 2-4 pm. We will give a short update on our work and show a video from 2-2:30. The rest of the time is just for fellowship. Please stop by and say hi if you are in the area. The address is 3508 Glade Rd. Colleyville, TX. 76053. (817-354-5757)

God bless you all.

Love,

Steve, Nancy, JT, Matthew, Ben and Katie

Guaranteed Two Phrases NEVER Before Uttered in the Same Sentence

— May 28, 2005

My life has had lots of surprises since 1998, but even my most optimistic friends would not have predicted this:

I won a full ride to Harvard.

You would not believe how NATURALLY this can be inserted into a conversation:

> Drive Through Window Guy: You want a double cheeseburger and a Diet Coke?
> Me: Did you say something about Harvard?
> DTWG: No.
> Me: I did get a full ride scholarship to Harvard.
> DTWG: Do you want fries with that?

We live in an age where people get too much information, so I don't mention that the class is only for a week, and that the scholarship was obviously based on need, not merit. Why overload people?

My wife, who the term `long suffering' was invented, has grudgingly accepted my plans to have t-shirts made for the whole family. She has drawn the line at tattoos.

Speaking of my dear one, her birthday is Monday May 30th. Would you call her on her cell and wish a happy birthday or email her? We go back to Kenya in about two months; it's MUCH cheaper to call her when we are here.

Your pal,

Steve

Greetings from Texas!
— *June 5, 2005*

This is Nancy writing for a change, and for a very special reason. Steve turns 50 on June 14 of this year.

Some of you receiving this have never even met him, but some of you know him well and have been touched, impacted, encouraged, or at least humored by him. On this half-century mark in his life, I would like to ask those of you who know him (and anyone else receiving this) to take a minute and send him a birthday greeting. Email or snail mail—either is fine. And you can do it now or wait until closer to his birthday, whenever you can remember!

In trying to think of the best possible way to bless Steve, this is what the Lord put on my heart. Steve really has no idea how many people he has encouraged over these past 50 years and I would love for him to become aware of some of the fruit of a life that is being well-lived. Let's give him an "It's A Wonderful Life" type birthday! In your greeting you might want to recount a situation when he encouraged you or a time he challenged you or even a time he made you laugh when you needed to!

Thanks so much for helping me bless Steve.

Nancy Peifer

Didn't You Used to be Steve Peifer? Adventures in Conferences and Conventions
— July 4, 2005

A dream came true in the last week, and it almost was a twofer.

I've been to a conference of Christian colleges, a seminar at Harvard, and an Oracle convention in the last few weeks. They have all been good, all in different ways.

The Christian conference was in Grand Rapids, Michigan. Living in a college dormitory was enlightening; it was hard to believe that so many good memories came from such an ugly place. College is really for 18 year olds; I was happy to be done with that stage of my life. It was a great conference, and an opportunity to tell many schools about RVA.

My secret dream was to attend one more Oracle convention while I was in the states. I work for the most elite Oracle consulting company in America, and they speak in an odd code that is not understandable for someone with my IQ. Truth is, when I was in the midst of technology, I was never much good at it, but osmosis did help. Being away from it so many years has caused me to sit on conference calls hoping that I will understand at least parts of some sentences.

So obviously, I would not be on the A-team for an Oracle convention. But owing to the miracles of geography, there was an Oracle convention in the town next to ours. My boss, who cures major diseases while flossing her teeth, managed to get me admitted to the floor.

I went to several sessions, which showed me how hopelessly out of it I really am. But then was the Rip Van Winkle moment. I was walking through the exhibitor booths, and someone asked me `Didn't you use to be Steve Peifer?'

That is actually a harder question to answer than you might think.

I got to celebrate my 50th with lots of friends, including one of my oldest friends who flew up from Connecticut. He is a Yale grad, so he was rather incensed about the whole Harvard thing, which he celebrated by giving me a Harvard shirt, pennant, pin and hat.

He wanted me to be PREPARED.

Harvard was amazing; it was so helpful in learning how to help the kids at RVA. I got to meet with legends in admissions, and I still can't believe I got to go.

Wednesday night was a free night, and they had tickets to the Boston Pops. One of my dreams in life was to see the Pops in concert.

And yell Freebird.

If you aren't an American, Freebird is an old rock song that gets requested at every concert in America. It was a dream to yell Freebird at a Pops concert.

But then I had a moral dilemma.

Debbie Boone was playing a concert in the hotel I was staying at. I don't know about you, but in the 70's I knew at least three jokes whose punch line was `Debbie Boone.' I found out there was a 10 pm show, so I would go to the Pops, run back, and have a Freebird twofer.

The Pops was fantastic, and I'm sure yelling Freebird showed my innate sophistication to those Boston hicks, but I have sad news to report on Debbie:

I was the only person to purchase a ticket to the 10pm show. They cancelled the show.

No Neil, and Debbie cancels. How much weight can one man bear?

Fortunately, Nancy got to fly up to Boston on a frequent flier ticket after the conference, and we celebrated 20 years of marriage. Some special friends had done so many special things to make it spectacular for us.

But just being with Nancy is pretty darn spectacular.

I missed Father's Day, and Katie called me and told me `A daddy should not be away from his precious girl today.' I've never been away from my kids on Fathers day before, and it was sad.

But Nancy and Katie picked me up at the airport, and she just couldn't stop grinning. It was the best father's day present ever, even if it was a bit late.

The twins turn four this week, and they are excited about seeing their first ever fireworks. As everything with them, it is all an adventure, and as you celebrate the fourth, be grateful for a country that welcomed our two little ones with open arms.

Your pal,

Steve

PS We will be speaking at Trinity Church in Cincinnati on July 10th at 9:30am and 11:15am. Please stop by and say hi if you are in the area. On July 11th, we will be at some old friends' house in Barrington Illinois at 7pm. Let us know if you'll be in the area!

PS We leave in thirty five days!

Your Pal, Steve

Achieving Success through Failure: A Year in America
— *August 7, 2005*

My marriage, the birth of my older children and the adoption of the twins use to be the happiest days of my life. I risk exposing my shallow side by revealing what is now, without question, the happiest day of my life.

The day the twins got potty trained is without a doubt the happiest day of my life. And you can say anything you want about the excesses of American capitalism, but without Care Bear panties, we would not have achieved this great victory, so God bless corporate America.

But it does lead me to a question that has been bugging me all year: Will someone explain to me the ad about the bear hugging the toilet paper? The only thing I can think of is how many rolls he will need, and I'm sure that wasn't the point of the ad, but American marketing just doesn't make sense to me anymore, so help me out, ok?

When I got on the plane from Kenya to America, I prayed that I would get closer to God. I had felt that I had been able to accomplish some good things, but I was just busy doing stuff. I wanted to get closer to God.

What I meant by that is that I would have longer quiet times, and in them, God would serve up a big load of Himself, and I would consume it somewhat in the manner of a large hot fudge sundae.

What I learned is to be more specific in how I prayed. I did grow closer to God this year, but it came from failing at almost everything I touched.

I got turned down by over one hundred foundations trying to get funding for computers and school lunches.

I worked part time for a wonderful company who paid me very generously for the work I did, but about the fifth time I was interviewing a consultant and one of the twins would plead: `Daddy, could you PLEASE give me a wipe?' was the day I realized I wasn't meant to work from home and that I was never very productive for them.

I really wanted to take my kids to Disneyworld, so I took a part time commission job which should have been a natural for me.

I didn't earn a single commission. We didn't go to Disneyworld.

I started and finished a masters in college counseling, but it was harder and took much more time than I ever expected. It ate up much of the time I hoped to use to see more of my friends.

In all my failure, I turned to the Lord and He met me in my despair. I grew closer to Him because of my failure. I am returning to Kenya as a different man. I am a broken man.

I discovered that my bottom line was that I liked writing the checks, but it was hard to receive monies. I didn't really want to depend on anyone.

And I failed. In the midst of it, I confessed my failings to Him, and He showed me that I needed Him and all my friends.

Which is Christianity 101 and should be obvious to anyone who has been a Christian as long as I have. But maybe the wonder of being 50 is wisdom will begin to thrust itself on me.

In all the failure, we still received the funding for 6-8 computer centers, and to increase the number of children we feed to almost ten thousand a day. I can't be anything but grateful for that. We didn't hit the goals we set, but we gave it our best shot.

I can't end this on a downer. There are so many people to thank that we won't thank anyone individually in this letter; it would be like a phone book. I would say we are grateful beyond words, but then my friend Ben Downs would gleefully give thanks that he found a way to shut me up.

I can't repay you all, but I do have something that I think is of value to share with you.

In Kenya, the sun rises at 6 am and sets at 6pm. There are no long summer nights.

I want to tell you: there is nothing better than an American summer. Going for walks with my children in the evening, taking the twins for their first fireworks and baseball game (Why do they all wear HATS?) and eating ice cream with Nancy was such a wonderful gift.

Life in America is so busy. Let this be my gift to you: there is nothing sweeter than an American summer. Take time to enjoy a little of it before it goes away.

Your pal,

Steve

Your Pal, Steve

Steve, Nancy, JT, Matthew, Ben and Katie returned to Africa
on August 8 2005 ...

and continue their mission ...

Please visit:

www.yourpal-steve.org

and

www.solutionbeaconfoundation

for more information.

All profits from the sale and distribution of this publication are used to support
the programs and the Peifers.

You can make a difference.

-- The Solution Beacon Foundation
December 2005

2367303

Made in the USA